# RC Ground School

The Beginner's Guide to Flying Electric RC Airplanes

Jim Mohan

# DEDICATION

To all the modelers who have shared their insights and knowledge with me over the years.

# CONTENTS

Preface ..................................................................................................................vi

1 Choosing a Plane ............................................................................................3

2 Choosing a Transmitter ..............................................................................17

3 Choosing a Simulator....................................................................................25

4 Joining the AMA and a Flying Club ........................................................31

5 Finding an Instructor....................................................................................35

6 Online Modeling Communities ..................................................................39

7 Operating Your Model ..................................................................................47

8 Model Safety..................................................................................................55

9 Where to Fly..................................................................................................59

10 Field Operations ........................................................................................65

11 Basic Aerodynamics for RC Pilots...........................................................75

12 Motor Basics................................................................................................87

13 Electronic Speed Control and Battery Eliminator Circuit Basics...........95

14 Battery Basics ...........................................................................................105

15 Propeller Basics.........................................................................................113

16 Receiver Basics.........................................................................................119

17 Putting Your Power System Together ......................................................125

18 RC Accessories .........................................................................................133

# Preface

## Why this book

Before starting this book, I did a quick search on RC flying on the big online booksellers. I was looking for some support materials for an online web course I've developed for folks getting started in flying radio control aircraft. My online course covers many of the topics a new pilot will need to be familiar with but not to the extent possible in a book or other long form resource. Many of the books in the search results were fairly old. Many dealt mainly with internal combustion engine powered models. There have been so many changes in the hobby, especially electric flight, that there seemed to be a need for an updated, electric-focused resource for beginners and those interested in converting to electric powered aircraft.

## Benefits

This book provides one primary benefit to the new modeler. Besides being written in a chatty, informal style, it presents many of the key topics a new modeler should be knowledgeable about in one place. There are a multitude of resources for someone who is willing to spend a lot of time searching. With this book, you can your spend time learning about key concepts instead. As your experience and interest in the hobby grows, you'll want to become familiar with some of those other information sources. Without some base level of knowledge, though, you'll likely end up more confused by the subtleties and opinions you'll find.

I try not to be prescriptive. In section one, for example, I offer no recommendation for your first RC model. I do offer a number of things you should consider when choosing a model. Ultimately, it is your choice and your investment. I simply outline some important criteria you should assess when making your choice. Each modeler's situation is a bit different.

## Focus on electric powered models

Glow and gas powered models have been around for decades. There are lots of books and resources for the new modeler who wants to go that route. A guidebook on glow powered models published 20 years ago will likely still be a relevant resource today. The story is different for electric models.

Most of the biggest changes in the radio control flying world involve electric powered models. In fact, a large proportion of the growth in model aviation can be attributed to electric powered models. I started flying my first electric model, a Multiplex Easy Star, a decade ago. I was one of only one or two people in a nearly 300 person club flying electric models. Today, in that same club, nearly 90% of the members fly electric models and may of those pilots fly electric models exclusively. That is not an unusual situation.

Technology advances in battery chemistry and an exploding market for batteries and small electric motors have driven prices down adding even more interest to the electric power corner of the hobby. One of the first lithium polymer batteries I purchased cost $50 on sale. Today the same size battery with greater discharge performance can be had for under $10. The same thing happened with motors and electronic speed controls. Components that cost $90 just a few years ago can now be had for $10 - $20. This trend has put model aviation within reach of a huge number of potential hobbyists.

## How to use this book

This book is divided into three sections. For many folks interested in learning more about flying radio controlled models their first questions will be about the airplanes and getting started. Section one addresses those questions. The chapters are designed to stand alone so readers can go directly to whatever topic interests them most. There is no need to read through the chapters in order. It is a good idea to give some thought to the selection criteria in each chapter before rushing out to purchase equipment, though. As you'll see, some topics overlap so decisions about planes can impact decisions about transmitters and so on.

Section two explores the key things a new modeler will need to know when operating his or her new aircraft. We'll approach these topics primarily from a safety stand point. Chapters will address safe model handling, selecting flying locations and typical field operations. A basic knowledge of these key points will help ensure you aren't chastised for violating safety rules or other common operational procedures.

Section three takes a deeper dive into how your model works and how to go about beginning your collection of tools and gadgets. This includes a beginner's guide to aerodynamics, power system components and important accessories for your field box. Modelers converting to electric power will find the information in the section helpful as they consider modifying some of their current models to use electric power.

# Section One

In this section we'll discuss those burning questions that people considering the hobby want answers to. We'll help you answer the questions:

What plane should I choose?

Should I join a club?

How can I find an instructor?

Can I teach myself to fly?

Should I choose new or used equipment?

# 1 Choosing a Plane

One of the first things beginners often want to think about is picking a plane. This is totally understandable but acting on this impulse too quickly often ends with a poor choice or a good choice that simply doesn't match the new pilot's circumstances. Every modeler you speak with will have an opinion on what makes a good first plane. Many times it will be the type of plane on which they learned to fly. If their needs and circumstances were the same as yours, then you'll probably be OK going with their suggestion. If not, you may be disappointed.

In this chapter, we'll look at some of the things you should consider before deciding on one of the many choices out there for trainer aircraft. Knowing what will fit your situation will help bring your choices down to a more manageable number.

Let's get started.

## Teaching Yourself to Fly

If you find yourself in a rural or remote area you'll discover the abundance of places to fly your model is offset by not having others to guide you along the way. Having an instructor can be a great asset as you begin your modeling career. Unfortunately, that may not be an option for you.

Don't worry! Lots of modelers have taught themselves to fly and recent technology advancements have made going down this path even easier. Let's take a look at several of them.

## Foam Airplanes

Probably the biggest technology impact has been the development of strong, durable and good looking foam models. Early foam models were molded out of EPS or expanded polystyrene foam. While these models looked great, the foam was brittle and crashes often resulted in small pieces of foam blowing across the runway or flying field like bits of popcorn. In those cases where the pieces were large enough to reassemble, special foam glue was required as one of the most common adhesives used in modeling, CA or cyanoacrylate, would melt the foam.

Figure 1.1. An E-flite Apprentice EPO trainer.

Most current foam models use EPO or expanded polyolefin foam. This foam is much stronger and denser than EPS foam allowing it to withstand much more abuse. Small dings and dents can sometimes be massaged out of the structure using your fingers and some hot water. Breaks and tears can be similarly reformed and glued together using CA. This is particularly important to the modeler who is teaching him or herself to fly. There will be some *oops* events. An EPO model is much more likely to be repairable.

The third type of foam used in model airplanes is known as EPP or expanded polypropylene foam. You will often find EPP foam used in profile-type models that are used for extreme maneuvering and ultra-fast flying wings. When used with carbon fiber rods and packing tape for support, these lightweight models are nearly indestructible. Unfortunately the extreme maneuvering and high speed these models are designed for don't lend themselves to a training role.

To close this section on foam airplanes we need to note that the models themselves are fairly inexpensive and in most cases spare parts are easy to obtain. Be sure to check your local hobby shop's or your online supplier's assortment of spare parts before deciding on which airplane is right for you.

## Simulators

Simulators are a great way to get some of the basics of RC flying down before taking your model airborne. We'll have a detailed discussion of simulators in Chapter 3 but for now let's look at the basics.

Simulators come in a variety of price ranges from free to a couple hundred dollars. If your goal is to simply learn the basics and you're on a budget, go with a free one. One of the most popular is called Flying Model Simulator or FMS for short. It has been around for a long time and has built up quite a collection of models you can choose to download and fly. This simulator can be used with a typical PC game controller that has two thumb type controller buttons. For basic orientation practice that is all you need. You can also purchase packages with USB RC controllers from several of the big online hobby shops. Packages in the $20 to $30 range are very likely FMS-based simulators. Read the product descriptions to make sure.

If money is not an issue, pricier packages are also available. Products such as Real Flight and Phoenix provide very realistic aerodynamics and excellent visual displays. The Phoenix package can be purchased with a 2.4 gigahertz RC transmitter which may help offset overall costs if you'll also be purchasing a radio.

Whether starting out frugal or jumping in with a top-of-the-line simulator, you should seriously consider getting an RC simulator – especially when teaching yourself to fly. A hundred crashes in the sim cost you nothing.

## Autopilots

One of the newer technologies on the market is the result of microelectronic components that sense attitude and acceleration. Let's discuss two of them.

The first are stabilization devices that plug into the aircraft's receiver or are sometimes built into it. These devices sense movements and make control inputs to counteract the effect of wind and turbulence. These devices have adjustments for each axis – roll, pitch and yaw. When properly set they help ensure the aircraft remains fairly stable allowing the pilot to focus on directing the aircraft rather than making lots of small corrections due to wind. These kinds of devices are available from several manufacturers and retailers. Some can be purchased individually and added to the model. Some models come with them preinstalled. Prices vary considerably by brand and features.

For the new pilot teaching him or herself to fly, one of the most interesting technology advances involves adding to the capabilities of the stabilizers described above. Horizon Hobby has several models equipped with what it calls SAFE® Technology. The electronics in these models allow the new pilot to program in limits to pitch and roll inputs. In beginner mode the movements are limited reducing the chance of over controlling the aircraft and ending up in an unusual attitude. In the intermediate mode the limits are expanded but still prevent wild gyrations. In the experienced mode, no limits are imposed. An optional panic mode allows the pilot to press a switch on the transmitter and have the aircraft return itself to straight and level flight assuming there is enough altitude to complete the maneuver. Flyzone has also released a trainer with similar electronic support it calls WISE™.

## Learning with an instructor

The social aspects of model aviation are an important draw for many joining the hobby. It's fun to have a group of people who share the same interests to talk with and share experiences. Most of the time that will mean joining a model airplane club. Two likely advantages of joining a club will be they have a place to fly and they will have experienced pilots who have been appointed to be club instructors.

Using a club facility provides you with an open area to fly that meets the requirements of the land owner, local government and other groups like the FAA who have input into model aviation.

Let's take a look at some things to consider when choosing to fly with an instructor.

## Taking things step by step

An instructor will be able to coach you along the way and provide you with needed background. Examples of this include using proper frequency controls at the RC field and using proper flying field procedures. Through explanations, stories and personal experiences, your instructor will be able to help you quickly master the basics of flight. He or she will be able to have you build your skills practicing basic maneuvers while handling some of the more complicated tasks themselves. As your skills increase, you'll be able to take on more and more of the flight phases until you solo.

Your instructor will also be able to teach you proper safety procedures used around model aircraft. Whirling propellers can and occasionally do cause serious injuries. Your instructor will be able to point out and insist that you develop a good safety sense when working around your model. This includes such things as not connecting your battery until approaching the flight station just before takeoff and not doing any maintenance on your bird requiring power with the propeller attached. We'll talk more about safety in section two of this book.

## Expanded first model choices

In the Teaching Yourself to Fly section we focused the discussion on foam models due to the likelihood of crashes, their easy repairs and available spare parts. If you choose to fly with an instructor at a club setting, you open up some additional choices when it comes to models. While everything discussed above regarding foam models still applies in a club setting, having an experienced instructor allows you to choose larger, more traditionally constructed models. These models are built from light ply, balsa and have a film covering.

Figure 1.2. A typical balsa and light ply trainer.

These larger, heavier models are easy to see and their mass allows them to deal with the wind better than light-weight foam models. Many have been modified by their manufacturers to use electric power while having a history of years and sometimes decades of successful training flights. These models become a more viable option when using an instructor. The issue here is their ability to be repaired.

We're going to assume your instructor will not allow you to get into a position where a crash is the likely outcome. While that can't always be prevented, a good instructor will be able to rescue you and your model from dangerous airborne situations. With these larger balsa and film models, a significant crash will likely result in the complete loss of the model. Unless you are coming with considerable model building skills, significant damage to a balsa and film model will be difficult to repair. This is not to say that these models are fragile or weak. That is certainly not the case. They will be able to withstand hard landings, ground loops and the like. Where they don't fare as well as a foam model is a full-on 30 to 90 degree nose down impact with the ground. As with foam models, check on the availability of spare parts when deciding on one of these trainers.

## Limiting your investment

If you are somewhat unsure whether flying model aircraft will be something you enjoy, learning to fly with an instructor in a club setting can be an economical way to find out. Many clubs have their own trainer aircraft instructors can use with people new to the hobby. That means you simply need to inquire at a local RC club about learning to fly and they will help set you up with an instructor who has access to a plane. Depending on the club, this may mean learning on a glow powered plane instead of electric but the flying skills transfer effortlessly. In some cases, the instructor may use his or her own plane so access to an electric powered model may still be easy.

The vast majority of model airplane clubs are chartered by the Academy of Model Aeronautics (AMA). This national body speaks for modelers in the political arena and lays out a national standard for safe model operations. AMA clubs require people who fly at their facilities to be members of the AMA. Recognizing that some potential members may want to 'try before they buy,' the AMA has what it calls the Introductory Pilot Program. Clubs who support this program will allow you to work with an instructor for up to 60 days without joining the AMA or the club. This will be plenty of time to see if you like flying model aircraft.

You can easily find an AMA chartered club by going to the AMA web site and clicking on the 'find a club' link on their home page (www.modelaircraft.org). You'll be able to search by zip code and distance. The search results will indicate whether the club has instructors and participates in the AMA Intro Pilot Program.

With the AMA Intro Pilot program and the use of club trainers and instructors, you can basically fly for free for two months while you decide if the hobby is right for you. You'll also be able to get to know more about what next steps will be right for you in terms of model and equipment purchases.

## Choosing your first airplane

There are several other things you should consider when choosing your first model in addition to the things we've already discussed.

## Design

When you look at the options for trainer-type aircraft, you'll notice two basic designs. For more traditional aircraft, you'll notice that trainers are high wing aircraft such as the full scale Cessna 172. High wing models are preferred over mid- or low-wing models as they are easier to control. With a high wing plane the model's center of gravity is below the wing. You'll also notice that the wings have an upward slant or bend to them. This bend is called dihedral. Planes with dihedral tend to return to wings-level flight when the flight controls are released. This is not the same as the self-righting electronics we discussed earlier. It simply means when the aircraft is in a 10 – 15 degree bank it will slowly move back to wings level if the flight controls are centered.

High wing trainers also provide the modeler with a plane that looks like a real plane. While the lines may not exactly match that of any full scale aircraft, it just looks right. Many high-wing trainers are modeled after full scale aircraft so they closely match their full scale counterparts.

The other common design option for trainer-type aircraft is a more glider-like model with a rear-facing motor behind the cockpit. For years the Multiplex Easy Star was one of the few models using this design. Now there are numerous similar foam models.

Figure 1.3. A Multiplex Easy Star glider style trainer.

These kinds of models have their wings mounted through the fuselage, not mounted on top. The wings are normally wide with turned up wingtips. This bend is the dihedral mentioned earlier. This wing configuration results in the self-leveling provided by dihedral and low wing loading. That is, the area of the wing is large compared to the weight of the model. This allows the model to fly very slowly giving the new pilot plenty of time to react. Since the motor is on top of the fuselage facing backward, you're much less likely to damage the motor or propeller on landing.

You can find both three and four channel versions of this model style. Three channel models use the rudder for banking instead of ailerons. Four channel models have ailerons. Four channel models will be a bit more maneuverable. The difference between three and four channels will not be as noticeable for this glider style model as it would be in a high wing trainer for basic maneuvers.

## Landing gear

A high wing trainer will very likely have landing gear. Part of what makes a high wing trainer look like a full scale airplane is having wheels. Glider style trainers are just as likely to not have landing gear. They are sometimes known as 'belly landers.'

As you might guess, there are some things you should consider when deciding on whether and what type of landing gear you want your model to have. With belly landers, it's easy. You simply give them a toss to take off and you skid to a stop upon landing. Belly landers are much less influenced by the wind on takeoff or landing. By that I mean, the pilot does not have to worry about cross winds as all he or she needs to do is face the wind and give the plane a toss or skid to a stop opposite whatever direction the wind is blowing. Belly landers are also advantageous when using a field with long grass. Long grass can be difficult for a model's wheels to roll through resulting in nose overs on takeoff or landing cartwheels when the gear gets hung up unexpectedly.

For trainers with landing gear there are two types. The most popular and easiest for new modelers to control are tricycle landing gear. Planes with tricycle gear have two main gear and a nose gear. This gear arrangement allows the aircraft to sit level on the ground. The nose gear is used for steering and because the plane's weight distribution keeps the nose on the ground until flying speed is attained, these planes are easier to control during takeoff. On landing, the pilot keeps the plane in a slightly nose high attitude as it settles onto the runway. Again, since the weight distribution is forward of the main gear, the nose will drop to the runway and the pilot steers the plane using the nose gear.

The other type of landing gear uses a tail wheel instead of a nose wheel. Tail wheel models, often known as 'tail draggers,' are more difficult to control on both takeoff and landing. When taking off, the pilot must manage the elevator control to keep the tail on the runway to take advantage of tailwheel steering until the rudder has enough airflow going past it to become effective. That is, to be able to cause the aircraft to rotate around the yaw axis. Cross winds, motor torque and something called 'p-factor' can cause the aircraft to veer from the desired heading. If the tail becomes airborne before the rudder is effective, the pilot will lose heading control on the takeoff. Not good. The same thing occurs on landings but to a lesser extent since the motor is usually at low power settings or off. If the pilot does not get the tail down soon enough, crosswinds and just uneven friction on the wheels will cause the model to veer to one side or the other. If the pilot adds back stick to pull the tail down with too much speed, the model will become airborne again. This is referred to as ballooning or a ballooned landing. This can often result in a stall and subsequent crash.

Figure 1.4. A HobbyZone Super Cub EPO trainer with a tail wheel style landing gear.

For most new modelers, if choosing a model with landing gear, a tricycle configuration will be the best choice.

## RTF vs. ARF

If you have done any model shopping at all, you have run across the abbreviations RTF and ARF. RTF stands for ready-to-fly and ARF stands for almost-ready-to-fly. Let's take a look at some things you should consider.

Ready to fly models come with everything the new modeler will need to fly the model. An RTF package will include a transmitter, all model electronics, a battery and a battery charger. The model itself will be almost completely assembled often requiring less than an hour to complete. The motor, speed control, receiver and servos will normally all be placed properly and connected. You will normally need to attach the tail or empennage and the wings. This may include connecting aileron servo leads to the receiver and attaching control pushrods to the tail surfaces. When it comes to getting into the air quickly, an RTF package can be a good choice.

The downside to RTF packages is that the transmitter and receivers may be house brands that aren't compatible with other brands or technologies. Additionally, things like the included charger will be an adequate but low cost, low capability device. It may also be difficult to find replacements for the transmitter or receiver should they break or become damaged. This will result in your purchasing new components for your model. Make sure you understand what brand the components in your package are and do a little detective work to see how easy replacements can be had.

Almost ready to fly models or ARFs do not include transmitters, receivers, batteries and sometimes not any electronics. ARFs built of balsa and ply with film coverings, often known as built-up models, usually include only the aircraft structure. This allows the pilot to choose the brand and size of components he or she wants. This obviously adds to the cost of the total purchase and can greatly increase the assembly time. With these models, you will need to mount the servos, place and attach pushrods, attach the tail or empennage, landing gear, motor, receiver and other parts. If you are handy or have an experienced helper, these models will greatly increase your understanding of your model and how everything works together.

ARFs molded from foam almost always include the servos already installed and properly mounted in addition to the fully installed motor and electronic speed controller (ESC). The motor and ESC are properly sized for the model to perform adequately. Servos are usually low cost, house brand versions. Foam ARFs require very little assembly. You will normally need to glue or screw on the empennage, attach the wings, mount the landing gear and connect some pushrods to the control surfaces. You will also need to mount your own receiver and provide your own battery. Refer to Chapter 18, RC Accessories, in section three of this book for more on chargers and other support tools.

If you intend to have more than one model, purchasing a name brand transmitter and a receiver for your ARF models is usually a more economical choice. You can use your transmitter for numerous models rather than ensuring you have both the model and the right transmitter packed when you go to the field not to mention the extra cost of single use transmitters. However, if you still have some doubts about how well you'll like flying model airplanes, an RTF package can be a good place to start.

## Outliers

There are always exceptions to the rule or common practice. For example, a very popular model new pilots use is the ParkZone T-28 Trojan. Normally, an experienced RC pilot would never recommend a warbird style model to a new pilot. With lots of power and a low wing, one would normally pass by the T-28 as a trainer even though it was used as a primary pilot training aircraft in its full scale glory. However, with its durable EPO construction, dihedral, light weight and easy access to spare parts the ParkZone T-28 can be a good choice for the new pilot.

Figure 1.5. A ParkZone T-28 Trojan

Other outliers might include models with advanced assistive technology that ease the burden on the new pilot.

## For Your Consideration

There are a great number of models that will get you off on the right foot. Here are several you should consider depending on your specific needs as we've discussed in this chapter.

If you are teaching yourself to fly in a large space:

**E-flite Apprentice S 15e with SAFE**. You can get this either as an ARF or RTF. If you are just starting out, the RTF version will work well as it includes a 5 channel basic Spektrum transmitter. If you have a line on a transmitter already, the ARF will save you a few dollars. The SAFE technology and EPO foam will help you as you teach yourself to fly.

**Flyzone Sensei FS EP with WISE**. You can get this either as an ARF or RTF. The RTF comes with a six channel basic Tactic transmitter. As with the Apprentice, if you have a line on a transmitter the ARF will be about $100 cheaper. Both Spektrum and Tactic have reasonably priced receivers, though the cheaper Spektrum receivers are normally third party brands.

**ParkZone T-28**. The T-28 comes in what is called Bind N Fly or Plug N Play versions. The difference is that the BNF version comes with a 6 channel Spektrum receiver. If you are planning on another transmitter brand go with the PNP version. It doesn't have the fancy stabilization systems but it is rugged and parts are easy to obtain.

**Hobby King Bixler 2**. The Bixler 2 has the classic Easy Star design with the motor facing rearward on the top of the fuselage. It looks like the Easy Star is getting hard to find. This Hobby King model comes in several versions including an RTF version with everything you'll need to get started. The down side to the RTF version is the transmitter and receiver are the Hobby King house brands. They will get you by with this model but without a lot of room to grow. Get the ARF version if you plan on another transmitter brand. You'll need an ESC too. That is a bit unusual for a foam ARF model but if you're ordering from Hobby King anyway, they have some suggestions with combo prices. This is the lowest priced suggestion.

**FMS Easy Trainer**. Like the Bixler, the Easy Trainer has the classic Easy Star design with the motor facing aft with big fat wings for slow speeds and good flight characteristics. The Easy Trainer comes in RTF and PNP or plug and fly versions. The PNP version will need a radio system, battery and charger. As with the Bixler RTF the downside to the RTF version is the house brand radio. Same advantages and disadvantages as listed above.

**HobbyZone Super Cub S with SAFE**. This model comes in both the RTF and BNF versions. The RTF comes with a Spektrum basic 4 channel transmitter. The BNF will require your own Spektrum transmitter. I listed this one last as it can be used in both a large space and a smaller area, too.

**HobbyZone Sportsman S+ with SAFE and Autoland**. The Sportsman S+ has the latest technology support. As it rolls out, it claims electronic support that will keep it in a defined space and has an auto land feature. This will rub many pilots the wrong way but if you are on your own, these extensive electronic support tools can be just what you need.

If you are teaching yourself to fly in a small space:

**HobbyZone Super Cub S with SAFE**. Discussed above. It will work in a small space too.

**HobbyZone Sportsman S+ with SAFE and Autoland**. Also discussed above. It also will work in a small space.

**HobbyZone Champ RTF**. This micro plane will work well in almost any back yard. It comes with a small transmitter that uses Spektrum's version of 2.4 GHz technology. This tiny model uses a single cell lipo battery as do several other micro models.

Flying with an instructor:

All of the models listed in the section on teaching yourself to fly in a large space apply when using an instructor in a large space or club setting. Each of those models are frequently seen at club fields. Here is another large field model. The difference is it is a balsa and ply model. You'll want the experience of an instructor while you build your skills.

**Great Planes Avistar Elite.** The RTF version of this model comes with a glow engine. Pick the ARF version and go with the electric power combo you can find on the Tower Hobbies website. You'll be choosing your own transmitter and receiver. Refer to Chapter 2 for an in-depth discussion on transmitter choices.

**House brand trainers.** Several hobby shops and online vendors have 'no name' high wing, balsa trainer ARFs. Your instructor may be able to guide you through selecting the power system and servos needed for one of these models. He or she may also be available to help you get it put together. As mentioned earlier, balsa ARF models entail considerably more assembly than do foam ARFs.

## Closing

This chapter has outlined a number of things you should consider when choosing your first model. Be honest with yourself and don't automatically go with the recommendation of another modeler. Getting some successful flights under your belt is critical to enjoying RC modeling. Frequent or expensive crashes have caused many to close the door to a rewarding hobby. By taking the things discussed here seriously, you'll get off on the right foot.

A final warning. Don't succumb to the temptation to get too much airplane to start with. Most experienced RC pilots will have a story about some new pilot showing up at the field with an expensive, advanced airplane which flies for about 10 seconds before transforming itself into a pile of kindling or foam popcorn. He or she is never seen again. Don't be that guy.

# 2 Choosing a Transmitter

Along with picking your first model airplane, you'll need to decide on a transmitter. As mentioned in the chapter on choosing a plane, if you go with an RTF or ready-to-fly package, your transmitter choice is predetermined. If not, however, there are a number of things you should consider. Let's take a look at some of those key factors.

## Channels

Model aircraft transmitters are usually grouped by the number of channels they can support. In this case, we're not talking about the frequency the transmitter uses but rather the number of components the transmitter can control. Each component has its own channel. Modern RC transmitters can control up to 18 and sometimes more aircraft functions. A transmitter that can control seven functions would be referred to as a seven channel radio. To control all seven functions on a particular model, the model would need at least a seven channel receiver.

For example, a basic transmitter will usually control four channels. These would include the throttle, ailerons, elevator and rudder. This is the basic set-up for trainer aircraft. Additional channels are used to control things like flaps and landing gear. As models become more advanced, the extra channels can also be used to control each aileron via its own channel allowing the up and down deflection to be individually adjusted to limit unwanted aerodynamic effects. Extra channels can also be used to allow multiple servos for the same control surface on larger models. An example of this might be servos for both the right and left half of the elevator.

If the budget can withstand the expense, consider a transmitter with six or seven channels. If not, pick a name brand four or five channel transmitter and start saving for your next upgrade.

## 72 MHz vs. 2.4 GHz

The Federal Communications Commission assigns radio frequency bands for different purposes to avoid radio interference. It assigned model aircraft operations to the 72 MHz band many years ago. This reserved space on the frequency spectrum is divided into 50 channels numbered 11 through 60. Radio controlled cars have a similar reserved range in the 75 MHz band. Licensed amateur radio operators also have reserved frequencies for model aircraft. In this section the word channel refers to the transmitter's frequency, not the number of components it can control.

Transmitters in the 72 MHz band can have fixed channels or may include replaceable frequency modules for different channels. Some modules can be set to transmit on any of the available channels.

The down side to 72 MHz band transmitters is that only one pilot at a time can use the channel without risking another model on the same channel crashing due to radio interference. Modelers often refer to this as getting shot down. To avoid this, model clubs use a frequency control board where only one person at a time uses the channel.

One of the biggest technology breakthroughs in transmitter technologies has been the shift to 2.4 GHz radios. As you might guess, these transmitters use the 2.4 GHz frequency band instead of 72 MHz Various manufacturers use different electrical methods but basically 2.4 GHz radios bind to the model's receiver and shift frequency within the band to automatically avoid interference. As a result, frequency control procedures aren't required and the possibility of being shot down is next to zero.

When it comes to new radios, almost all transmitters sold today are 2.4 GHz radios. Even house brand radios included with inexpensive ready-to-fly model packages are 2.4s. What this 2.4 GHz popularity also means is that if you have a 72 MHz radio there is little competition for your channel.

## New vs. Used

RC transmitters are fairly reliable electronic devices. When you match that with the fact that people leave the hobby due to a variety of circumstances, there are usually lots of transmitters for sale on eBay or Craigslist. In many cases, if you take advantage of an RC club's Introductory Pilot Program, your instructor may be able to connect you with a club member who has an older 72 MHz radio he'll be willing to give you. A member of a club I'm associated with posted a picture online of all the radios he and his dad had. There were at least two dozen in the photo. Folks like that are usually more than willing to give a transmitter to a new modeler.

You will also be able to find used transmitters for sale that are fairly new. These transmitters may be available because an experienced modeler moved from seven to nine or even 18 channels. It could also be that a senior modeler passed away leaving his gear to the club or a surviving spouse to sell or give away. Regardless of the reason, good used transmitters are not hard to find. Often times there will be a certified repair person nearby. In that case, you can let them go through the radio to ensure everything is working as it should. The radio's manufacturer may also have a repair or tune-up service available if you mail in your transmitter.

New transmitters are available through local hobby shops as well as numerous online hobby shops and vendors. Look around a bit. It is not unusual for hobby shops to carry only one or two brands of transmitters. Take advantage of the comments on the various RC message boards regarding the features and quirks of various transmitter brands and models. RCGroups.com and RCUniverse.com are two of the biggest online RC communities. See Chapter 6 for more on online modeling communities.

If you find a transmitter that has the number of channels you need and the features you want, you'll do well from a quality perspective with the major brands. Airtronics, Futaba, Hitec, JR and Spektrum have all been around for a long time. Newer brands such as FlySky, Tactic and Turnigy produce reasonable products at very reasonable cost. Some "off brand" transmitters use open source software supported by hobbyists so you can feed your inner geek if you are a hacker or coder.

For both new and used transmitters, be sure to assess the availability of receivers. Third party Spektrum compatible receivers can be had for as little as $7- $8. A seven channel Futaba brand receiver can cost about $70. Give some thought as to whether you want to be swapping out receivers from model to model or if each of your models will be getting its own. Also assess whether you are comfortable with low cost third party receivers or whether you feel better with brand-matched devices. When you know the answer to those questions, you'll have a couple of other variables to assess when choosing your transmitter brand.

## Basic vs. Computer

The lowest cost RC transmitters are basic models. By that I mean that they have all the basic controls for a model with that number of channels. The controls include the flight controls, perhaps a gear or flap switch, manual trims for the flight control levers and mechanical switches to reverse the servo directions or select a V-tail or elevon controls for those types of models. Basic transmitters can be used with more than one model but the servo directions and trims will need to be reset when changing from one model to another. In most cases, transmitters included in RTF packages will be basic models.

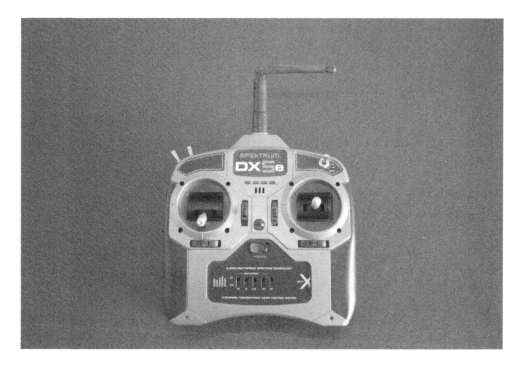

Figure 2.1. A basic 2.4 GHz 5 channel transmitter.

Basic transmitters are usually limited to 5, perhaps 6 channels. Basic four channel transmitters are common. A basic transmitter is usually a good choice for the new modeler. You should, however, give some thought to your next radio. In so doing, you'll have a target brand identified and be able to avoid having incompatible receivers for the new transmitter and feeling like you wasted your money. For example, if you were to get a basic five channel Spektrum brand transmitter and receivers then graduate to a 10 channel Futaba transmitter, your Spektrum receivers wouldn't work with your new radio.

Computer transmitters are so named because they are very complex computerized devices with extensive user selectable options and variables. You will know you are looking at a computer transmitter if it has an LCD screen on the front with a variety of menu and selection buttons.

Computer transmitters usually start with at least six channels. The computer programming within the transmitter allows the pilot to change or configure numerous settings electronically instead of using the mechanical switches used on a basic transmitter.

Here is just a small list of the variables you can set on the typical computer radio:

- Wing type
- Servo mixes (e.g. adding up elevator when flaps are lowered)
- Servo reversing
- Servo end point adjustments
- Flap deployment (both degree deflection and which switch controls it)
- Differential aileron deflection
- Servo sub trims
- High and low rates
- Exponential curves for control surfaces (Non-linear servo movement when control sticks are moved -- e.g. small servo movements close to center with larger movements at the end of the control range or vice versa)

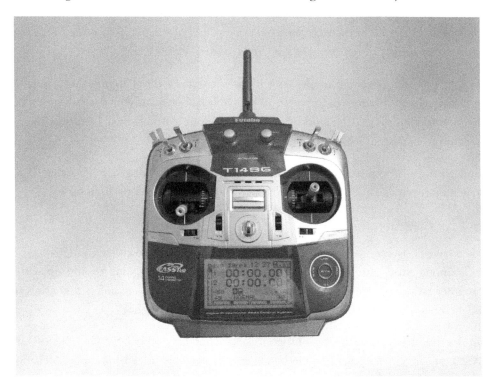

Figure 2.2. A computer transmitter. Note the LCD screen used for programming.

Some transmitter brands include large numbers of model memories in the transmitter. You must program each model into the transmitter the first time you plan to fly it. This allows you to simply select the model the next time you fly knowing that the proper servo settings, trim settings and other variables are right for the model. You won't have to reset anything. Spektrum transmitters even remember the code from the model's receiver and match it with the model's name the pilot has assigned to a memory position. If the code doesn't match, the receiver and transmitter won't pair. This prevents you from accidently flying model A with model B's variables dialed in. Such an error can result in a very exciting and short flight!

If you stay with the hobby very long, you'll upgrade to a computer radio. If the budget allows, getting more radio than you need is not a bad strategy. You'll grow into it.

## Modes

When you shop for a transmitter you'll probably notice radios labeled as mode one or mode two. These labels refer to the way the controls are assigned to the control sticks. Mode one radios use the left stick to control elevator and rudder. The right stick is used to control the ailerons and throttle. Mode two radios use the left stick to control throttle and rudder. The right stick controls the ailerons and elevator. The mode two configuration is like the controls on a full scale plane. Mode two is also the mode used by the vast majority of modelers in the United States.

There is no right or wrong mode. As with any psychomotor skill, practice with either mode is required. As a new modeler, you'll probably be better off with a transmitter mode common to your part of the world. Use the mode your instructor will likely be using. In the United States, that will be mode two.

Some advanced computerized radios allow the modes to be changed. Such a change will likely require a mechanical adjustment to the radio as well as a software input.

## For Your Consideration

If you have chosen to go with a name brand transmitter to start with, consider choosing from among these entry level computer transmitters. You're going to end up with a computer radio at some point so you might as well start with one unless you are really budget limited or truly uncertain about model aviation as a hobby.

**Futaba**. Futaba systems can be a bit confusing. They have FHSS, S-FHSS, FASST and FASSTest systems for sale. For the beginner, a reasonably priced full range, 6 channel system would be the Futaba 6J S-FHSS system. Receivers for this transmitters are reasonably priced and some high end Futaba transmitters are downwardly compatible so your S-FHSS receivers will still work if you go with a higher end transmitter later.

**Hitec**. Hitec Flash 7 seven channel radios have an interesting twist. You can get one of these beginner-level computer radios that will connect with Hobbico's SLT receivers sold under the Tactic brand. This opens up a large number of low priced receivers along with transmitter ready models. You'll need to select a transmitter paired with either the Hitec Optima or Maxima line of receivers.

**Spektrum**. The Spektrum DX6 and DX6i 6 channel computer radios are solid choices for the beginning modeler who wants room to grow. The more expensive DX 6 is capable of receiving telemetry data from the model while the DX 6i is not. The DX 6 also has a larger model memory and other more advanced features as it is the newer version of Spektrum's 6 channel transmitter. Review the specifications to see whether the additional cost is worth it to you. Several third party receiver choices make Spektrum a good choice for those planning on a hangar full of small models.

**Tactic**. Tactic transmitters make use of the SLT system mentioned above. Tactic has both 6 and 8 channel computer radios and since they fall in the low cost category, the Tactic 8 channel computer radio is a good choice as it is only slightly more expensive than its 6 channel brother. Tactic transmitters allow easy connection to Hobbico's line of transmitter ready models and Tactic receivers are reasonably priced. Tactic transmitters are the lowest priced of what most would consider 'name brands.'

## Closing

Choosing a transmitter will take some research and self-assessment. Your transmitter will be one of the most expensive and critical parts of your modeling tool box. By looking at some of the items discussed above you should be able to map out a plan that allows you to grow into the hobby without a lot of backtracking and wasted money.

A hand-me-down transmitter and receiver can be an excellent place to start. By the time you've mastered your first model you should be better positioned to answer some of the questions presented here as you think about an upgrade.

If budget is not a big issue and you plan on buying a new transmitter, spend some time researching and talking to other modelers to determine what the channel sweet spot will be for you. Having an 18 channel transmitter with no planes needing more than seven channels is a waste. Getting a brand new six channel transmitter then purchasing a seven channel airplane months later is also wasteful.

As someone new to the hobby, you simply don't have to spend hundreds of dollars on a transmitter. You'll have plenty of opportunity for that as your interest and skills expand.

# 3 Choosing a Simulator

A radio controlled model simulator can be an excellent investment for the new modeler. Sims, as we'll call them, are a great way to get the hang of flying a radio controlled model without risking the model itself. Crashes in the computer are cheap. That can't always be said in the real world. This becomes even more important if you are teaching yourself to fly out behind your house or at that nice big pasture your neighbor allows you to use. Let's take a look at some of the things you should consider when deciding on a sim.

## Fidelity

As someone who has hundreds of hours in full scale military simulators I can tell you that your sim's required level of fidelity is somewhat dependent on how you plan to use it. The highest level of fidelity is not always needed. Two of the components on which you'll need to assess fidelity are the visual subsystem and the aerodynamic engine. While computer coding techniques may integrate some of these tasks, this simplified conceptual version of simulator operations will help you wrap your mind around a very sophisticated piece of software.

## Graphics

Modern personal computers have amazing graphics. Even medium priced personal computers and flat screen monitors can product high definition images in a moving, fluid fashion. When one adds an additional graphics card with additional memory and computing power the images can be out of this world. Software designers work to keep up with the graphic capabilities of these computers and develop amazing flying sites and virtual worlds for you to fly your models. Other designers develop very detailed models to use in these sims. These models will show flight control movements, gear and flaps extending and retracting, and fun-to-watch crash sequences where parts go flying everywhere.

If you are just using the sim to learn to master aircraft orientation and how to control your model while both moving away from you and coming at you, some of this fidelity is overkill. In this case, a free or inexpensive sim will meet your needs from the visual fidelity perspective. A free or inexpensive sim will also work fine if you have an older computer that isn't quite powerful enough for the latest version of a top-line sim.

On the other hand, if you plan to jump into 3D flight or advanced aerobatics with several models on your shopping list, a high fidelity visual system may be a better choice. As with most things in the hobby, your budget will play a role in your decision.

## Aerodynamics

Your simulator's aerodynamics engine is probably the most important part of the sim. It is the part of the software that does the modeling of the physical forces interacting with your model. First, it uses the weather and other natural variables you set in the simulator. Many sims will allow you to specify wind speed and direction, field elevation, temperature and other elements that are important to how your model flies. Then the aerodynamics engine reads the physical characteristics of the model itself and computes the outputs based on things like control deflection, thrust, wing type and drag.

These are terribly complicated mathematical calculations. A great deal of your computer's processing power will be used to maintain a real-time, ever changing set of outputs to drive the graphics system which displays the results of your inputs on the screen. At the same time, the software is also computing your position over the ground in this virtual world causing the scene to shift as you fly.

How your model 'feels' in flight is due in large part to the quality of the aerodynamic engine. The test for a high quality aerodynamic engine in your simulator is when you can go out to the field and fly the actual, physical model of what you've been practicing on in the sim and feel like there is little to no difference.

As with the graphic system, the required fidelity of the aerodynamic engine is also dependent on how you plan to use the simulator. You won't need a $300 - $400 simulator to learn to go up and down or left and right. Free and inexpensive simulators will do those things just fine. If your budget is tight, there are more important things to spend your money on during your new-guy phase.

## Physical

Physical fidelity has to do with the actual controls you use to operate the simulator. In a full scale military or airline simulator, the pilot climbs into a mock-up of an actual cockpit where all the buttons and dials work just like they do in the real aircraft. With our RC simulators, the primary physical element for the sim will be the controller.

The free and basic simulators will allow you to use controllers as simple as a PC game-pad type controller. As long as it has two thumb pad levers, you're good to go. This situation would be considered a low physical fidelity situation. The game pad doesn't have the same size and shape of an RC transmitter and the thumb pads are usually self-centering which is not the case on the left stick of a mode two transmitter.

Inexpensive simulator packages often include a USB type transmitter box with the size and feel of an RC transmitter. In this case, the physical fidelity increases.

Advanced simulators often offer the pilot some choices. They may include a mock transmitter, an actual transmitter that can be used with real models or a cable that allows you to connect to your primary transmitter through the trainer port. Each of these choices ups the physical fidelity of your sim. Fortunately, physical fidelity is probably the least important variable for your simulator. A PC game controller will be fine for mastering orientation, turns and up and down.

Figure 3.1. Screen shot of E-flite Apprentice in the Phoenix RC simulator

## Advanced Features

Top-of-the-line simulators have some features that the free versions don't have or have with only basic capabilities.

If you are a person who enjoys online gaming, investing in a top-of-the-line simulator may be something to consider so you can make use of the social aspects of the software. Advanced simulators such as Real Flight and Phoenix allow you to join virtual fly-ins with modelers from all over if you have a good internet connection. If winter weather limits your flying time or if you are flying by yourself due to your geography, these virtual fly-ins can be a way to simulate club flying and get to know other modelers.

Advanced simulators will also include tools that allow you to model you own aircraft and flying sites. Many of the models available for your simulator may have come from other simulator enthusiasts who worked through the process of building a virtual model of either a home built aircraft or an actual model or full scale aircraft. These advanced tools also provide you the ability to modify existing models by changing their size or available power. Other modelers use the tools and their interest in photography to model where they fly in real life. In so doing, they are able to use the visual cues they have at their flying field to make simulator practice more life-like and precise.

Advanced simulators often include instructor modes. Using this feature, you are able to use a virtual instructor to explain and demonstrate both basic and complex maneuvers. This feature will likely include a small image of the transmitter with stick positions highlighted as well as audio or video instruction and fully automated demos of whatever maneuver is selected. Virtual instructor modes are very helpful if you are teaching yourself to fly.

## Practice

It is not unusual for some experienced, older modeler to comment on how quickly a teen or pre-teen pilot develops excellent flying skills. Such comments often include statements about how young people pick things up so quickly. While that might be true to some extent, another factor is practice.

On several occasions I've heard the teens at the field I use talk about going home and getting online with their sims. In speaking with their parents, it's not unusual to learn that these expert pilots spend lots of time practicing. Whether using a basic, inexpensive sim or one of the top-of-the-line best sellers, practice is the key to success.

When practicing with a simulator, you'll get the most from your time if you develop a flight plan for each practice mission. Focus your attention on some aspect of the flight. Early on, you may want to practice left turns while keeping the model fairly close within your virtual flying site. Next, add right turns. Then mix them up. Practice climbs and descents at various power settings. Next, focus on takeoffs or landings. Really work at them. While you may want to reserve some time to just play around, don't spend too much time just playing. Remember that it is not practice that makes perfect, its perfect practice that makes perfect. Spend most of your time doing things as perfectly as you can.

## Simulator Choices

Having given some thought to the important features you will need in a simulator and what features aren't important to you – at least right now; what are your choices? As was mentioned in the simulator section of Chapter 1, Choosing a Plane, you've got three basic choices.

The low-cost choice is to download Flying Model Simulator from one of several sites on the internet. This user-developed simulator is free, has lots of available models and has reasonable graphics and aerodynamic response. You can find instructions on building controller cables or simply use a PC game pad controller.

Next on an increasing cost curve is to purchase a basic simulator in the $19 to $50 range. These simulators come with a simulated transmitter box that will plug into your computer's USB port. The software is most likely the same FMS software mentioned above. You're basically paying for the controller.

A stripped down version of premium packages is the next choice. Real Flight offers basic packages of their top-of-the-line product for about $100. They don't include all the bells and whistles of their full-featured big brother but they provide excellent graphics and aerodynamics.

Top-of-the-line simulators are your fourth choice. Simulators such as Phoenix and Real Flight start at about $130 and go up to just over $200. The price difference is driven by the controller option you choose. Versions with just a cable to connect to your actual transmitter or versions with transmitter mockups are at the low end of the range. Versions with actual transmitters cost more.

The products we've discussed are well known and popular. You can find a fairly lengthy list of other simulator products in the Wikipedia article entitled RC Flight Simulator. You can also get some good user input by searching through the simulator threads at the RC Groups or RC Universe online communities.

## Closing

You should seriously consider getting an RC simulator. How much you spend on the software will depend on some of the things discussed in this chapter. If you have a club nearby and lots of good flying weather, you'll probably do well with a free or inexpensive sim. If you are teaching yourself to fly, then one of the advanced simulators may be worth the extra cost. Their built-in instructor functions and online fly-ins can be great for building your enthusiasm about the hobby along with your skills.

If you are unsure, get a free or inexpensive sim and try it out. You won't have much invested and upgrading is easy.

# 4 Joining the AMA and a Flying Club

One of the things I've mentioned already has to do with joining the Academy of Model Aeronautics and an AMA chartered radio controlled airplane club. It is a topic big enough to demand a bit more explanation. In this chapter we'll look at some of the things you should consider before ruling joining either in or out.

## The AMA

As stated on their website, the Academy of Model Aeronautics is an organization of modelers 'whose purpose is to promote development of model aviation as a recognized sport and worthwhile recreational activity.' The AMA supports all aspects of model aviation. It provides plans to model building enthusiasts, supports a variety of modeling competitions, provides supplemental liability insurance to members and more recently, it has become the primary voice advocating for modelers in the face of increasing threats of government regulation. Similar organizations exist in other countries.

## RC Clubs

For most modelers AMA membership provides two big advantages. First is the opportunity to join with other modelers in an AMA Chartered RC club. RC clubs who affiliate with the AMA agree to abide by AMA safety standards and to operate according to a set of principles. These include such things such as non-discriminatory membership policies. AMA clubs are also provided with liability insurance for flying related incidents. This insurance is a very valuable tool when negotiating flying field agreements with local governments or land owners.

Like most organizations, local RC clubs vary a great deal in their culture and the aspects of model aviation they support and value most. Some clubs are made up mainly of sport fliers who enjoy flying and socializing. Others focus on hosting events and competitions. For these modelers, competition is a very important part of the hobby. Others may focus more on helicopters than fixed-wing aircraft. The people involved in clubs also vary in openness and friendliness. Some clubs are very welcoming to new folks while others take a while to 'warm up' to new folks. With that in mind, you may want to visit several local clubs to see which one feels best to you.

For the new modeler, a local RC club will normally provide you with access to experienced pilots to teach you to fly. Previously, we mentioned the AMA Introductory Pilot Program. Clubs who support this program will allow you to fly for up to 60 days with a designated instructor without joining the AMA or club. Other clubs have their own training programs. In both cases, their goal is to help you develop your piloting skills quickly and safely.

## Individual Benefits

The other big advantage to AMA membership is the benefits directed at the individual member. The first benefit most mention is AMA liability insurance. Each member receives a 'per occurrence' coverage limit of $2,500,000. As with all insurance policies the limits are divided up into certain categories so be sure to review the insurance documents on the AMA website, www.modelaircraft.org. This insurance is also known as excess insurance which means it pays only after your individual liability insurance from your homeowners or renters insurance is exhausted. AMA insurance also has provisions for Accident/Medical coverage and Fire, Vandalism and Theft Coverage. Again, review the policy documents for coverage specifics.

While the insurance coverage is often the first benefit mentioned, it is hardly the only benefit of membership. Members also receive a monthly magazine called *Model Aviation* devoted to – well – model aviation. Members also gain access to all sorts of modeling resources as well as the ability to fly at AMA club fields and at AMA sanctioned events. AMA affiliated clubs require pilots to be AMA members.

Recently, moves by the United States Federal Aviation Administration or FAA to regulate model aircraft flying have concerned model aviation enthusiasts. The AMA has taken the leading role to engage with and inform the FAA about model aviation and to advocate for maximum flexibility for model hobbyists. This has become an increasingly important aspect of the AMA's service to modelers.

With the growing popularity of small foam models, the AMA recognized that there are folks for whom RC club flying may not be important. Reaching out to these 'park flyers,' the AMA developed a Park Flyer membership category which includes insurance coverage and access to AMA resources. It also provides modelers with a quarterly magazine and important information about operating their models safely. The AMA can also help with dealing with local governments to allow flying these small models in local parks.

An AMA Park Flyer membership for those with small electric models and who don't fly at an RC club site is a worthwhile investment. In many cases, you don't know what you don't know. Resources provided with this membership level can help get you informed on the issues and operating procedures to ensure safe model operations.

## Closing

AMA membership is a given if you plan to fly in a club setting. You can join online. Your receipt is enough proof to join a club and fly at their field in most cases. Your AMA membership card will arrive in the mail within a week or two. Many of your AMA member materials are online. You'll be able to find a membership manual and newcomers guide in the AMA documents section of the AMA website.

If you aren't planning on flying at a club site or if there aren't club sites nearby, AMA membership is still worth considering. The liability insurance applies whether you are flying at a club site or not. The AMA magazine is also a valuable resource for modeling articles, new product reviews, modeling related issues and of course advertisements from some of modeling's biggest vendors and providers. Take some time to review the AMA website to see for yourself.

# 5 Finding an Instructor

We've already discussed engaging an RC club instructor to help you get started. So in a sense, some of the information in the chapter will be a bit repetitive. There will be some new stuff, too.

## RC Club Instructors

If you were to show up at an RC club and ask someone to help you get started, the chances are high that most pilots you approach will say yes. RC pilots are often willing to share their knowledge and experiences. However, you may not know whether their flying skills are up to the task. Unfortunately, new pilots have stood in horror and frustration as their 'instructor' failed to recover their aircraft and it crashed in a cloud of dust and broken parts. In other cases, new pilots have paired up with harsh demanding pilots who made the learning experience more of a gauntlet of abuse than a partnership in learning.

Here are some ways to help avoid such experiences.

First and most important, visit the club site and talk with club members. Are they friendly? Do they fly the kinds of airplanes you are interested in? Are they experts practicing for the next big contest or sport flyers just out having fun? Are there pilots your own age or are they much older or younger? If there are several clubs within a reasonable distance, visit those too. Get the best sense you can about whether the club culture is one you will enjoy.

When you've decided on a club, speak with one of the club leaders about their instructor program. You can check the AMA website to see if the club you're considering has an instruction program or if it participates in the AMA Introductory Pilot Program. Use the 'find a club' link. Ask some questions about the instructors to help ensure a good fit with your needs. Will he use your model, his own or club trainers? Does he fly electric, glow or gas models? What is his availability? How many students has he trained? Does the club have a new pilot curriculum or does each instructor manage student progress against his own standards? Does he seem friendly? Strict? Demanding? Encouraging? Is there a she instructor?

When you have the answers to these and any of your own additional questions you're ready to pick an instructor and schedule lessons.

Figure 5.1. An instructor and student pilot using a wireless buddy box system.

## AMA Introductory Pilot Program

As discussed earlier, the AMA Introductory Pilot Program is a program that local clubs can choose to participate in. The advantage to using an AMA Intro Pilot is that you can fly at the club field, with an Intro Pilot without joining the AMA for up to 60 days. While in the program, your instructor's AMA insurance will cover you allowing you to use the club's facility. This way you can give model aviation a try without a big investment. As described in the program documents on the AMA website, the program is not a substitute for the club's normal training program for new pilots who are AMA members. Your Intro Pilot will likely take you through the same training program used by new pilots who have already joined the AMA. This program is primarily about insurance protection.

## Your local hobby shop

Your local hobby shop can also be a good source for instructor pilots. They may have someone on their staff who can act as instructor either with or without an additional fee. Obviously, you'll want to purchase your model from that shop if you plan on using one of their staff resources as an instructor. In other cases, they'll know local modelers who have taught others to fly. These modelers may be club instructors so the discussion on RC club instructors still applies. In other cases, they may simply be park flyers who have helped other park flyers master their models. As with the RC club instructors, meet with the person and ask some questions to see if he or she will be a good fit for your needs and learning preferences.

## Virtual Instructors and YouTube

You may have a very good virtual instructor available to you through your choice of simulator. Virtual instructors can be very helpful in mastering both the basics as well as more complex maneuvers. Demos, audio and video, and control stick movement displays can do much of what a real-life instructor can do. When you pair that up with a model with advanced stabilization electronics, you may be able to master your model with little to no assistance.

Another great learning tool is YouTube. You can find videos produced by not only other modelers but also manufacturers and vendors. These videos can provide you with a wealth of information on products and techniques. You can generally trust information from commercial sources. Read through the comments section on user videos for hints on whether that video producer knows what he or she is talking about. Unfortunately since video owners can screen comments, it's not a foolproof method.

## Closing

Choosing an instructor can be one of the most important decisions you can make. If you plan to use your instructor for more than 'stick and rudder' coaching it is important to find a well-informed person who will be able to give you good advice as you get started on your modeling adventure. If you like to do a lot of your own research or have already decided on your way forward, then an instructor with good flying and training skills will probably be enough.

Whether part of a club's training program or just a new friend at the park, having an instructor to help get your started safely and within the rules of the location you choose to fly is a good starting point. Given the choice of having an instructor or not – choose the instructor.

# 6 Online Modeling Communities

One of the best tools available to the new modeler are online communities specializing in modeling. The two largest and well-known are RC Groups and RC Universe. RC Universe has a related community specializing in electric models called Watt Flyer. RC Groups has a URL that will take you to the electric flight area within their groups. Use www.ezonemag.com. The other two sites can be accessed at www.rcuniverse.com and www.wattflyer.com.

There are a number of other communities available too. Those are often set up by vendors and used as a kind of crowd-sourced customer service site. You can ask questions about the products sold by that vendor and others who use them can respond as will vendor representatives. These sites are more narrowly focused as compared to the general sites mentioned above.

Online communities just like physical, geographical communities tend to have their own cultures. There are even subcultures within the groups depending on the topics. Your best bet is to explore several of these sites and decide which one best meets your needs. Most modelers will join several communities and after a while will discover they are spending most of their time on one site or another.

## How online communities work

Online communities are normally composed of three parts. The community's home page will often have content provided by the community owners and paid contributors. These articles may be about events around the nation or reviews of new products. The second and largest part of the community is the message forums. Each community will have dozens of major topics each with hundreds if not thousands of message threads. Each thread starts with a subject related to the sub-forum's topic and is followed by responses and comments by community members with something to add. The third part of the community is advertising. Most communities are free and they have to pay the bills. Click on the links to interesting products to learn more and help generate some income.

## Member Accounts

Most communities will allow you to explore the site as a guest. To participate in the conversations and make use of some of the forum tools, however, you'll have to register. Again, most communities are free but you'll need to establish a user name and provide some additional information such as the city, state and country where you live. Many modelers use cute or clever user names within the community. Your user name will be attached to your posts so keep it clean and short. Friendly folks will respond to your posts using your user name so don't make them type 50 characters just to get started. Take note of the user names when out exploring and you'll get some ideas. Many user names will include odd spellings or numbers as once a name is claimed it can't be duplicated. With thousands of members in some communities, you'll need to be creative.

RC Groups uses the location information to add a line in the post telling you how far away the users are from you. RC Universe and Watt Flyer publish the location info in the post. With this information you can set up some flying rendezvous with forum friends who are close by or located where you might be traveling.

Your member account section may also allow space for you to publish blog comments or post photos of your models. Folks who find your comments insightful and helpful can click on your user name and view the blog and photos.

## Forum Tools

Members have access to a variety of forum tools. The most helpful of these are search tools. These tools allow you to search for message threads dealing with what you are interested in. These search tools can be used to search the entire forum database or just search the message thread you're following. For example, you might search the entire community looking for information about the Apprentice trainer. You can search the entire community looking for that keyword and then when you find a specific message thread or two, you can go to those threads and search within each one to look for something specific. Search is a very powerful, timesaving tool.

There are also other thread tools besides search. Once you find an interesting message thread you can subscribe to it. Thread subscribers will receive email summaries of thread activity each day. That way you can keep up with the action on the thread via email without having to log into your browser. Other tools include showing a printable version of the page, sharing the page with someone else via email and one I really like, showing all the photos and other attachments community members have attached to their posts.

Popular message thread can be hundreds of pages long and include thousands of posts. These tools make it easy to zero in on what you are looking for.

If you find you have a question or specific comment to direct at only one community member, you can make use of forum software's private messaging function. For example, if you are responding to an item in a 'For Sale' thread, you'd probably use a PM. You wouldn't want to broadcast your phone number or payment information to others beyond the person you're purchasing from.

## Forum Etiquette

Different communities have different cultures and different etiquette. Some things are fairly common across communities, though, so let's take a look at some of them.

Most people come to the thread to learn something or to have a friendly interaction with other modelers. Occasionally, someone will write something that others disagree with. That is all part of the game. How one responds is important. Name calling, shouting using all capital letters and other abusive language is always inappropriate. Flame wars between two or three people on a message thread ruin the experience for the sometimes hundreds of others viewing the thread. In one case I witnessed, the animosity got so great and the language so coarse that the community moderator locked the thread. In other cases, users have been removed from the community under the terms of the user agreement.

One of the sayings around internet-based communities is abbreviated as DFTT. It stands for 'don't feed the trolls.' Trolls are people who can't say anything nice and always have something to criticize. The best way to deal with them is to ignore them. If you don't respond to their posts, it stops being fun and they move on.

Thread participants enjoy helping others and can develop a real sense of ownership in the thread. A common breach of etiquette is for someone to join the thread and say something like, "Can someone answer this question? I don't have time to look back through the thread to see if it has been asked before." Such questions may or may not be answered. Oftentimes they will be responded to with a not-so-subtle jab about being lazy. What the questioner is really saying is that their time is worth more than other community members'. It comes across as arrogant. Use the search. If you can't find it, then ask.

Off topic posts are another annoyance that may invite a reminder to move to the appropriate thread. There may be a temptation to post something totally off the thread's topic because you know the thread is very active with lots of participants. Don't do it. An occasional off topic post will likely go unremarked upon, but a new conversation within the thread will be called out. It is like having a sidebar conversation during a business meeting. It is poor form. If it's a topic you find interesting, start your own thread.

If you have found a product that you use that applies to the topic, recommending it and providing a link can be a helpful post. If you are linking to your website where you sell the product, that's out of bounds. Promoting your own products is generally a no-no. If you have a product to sell, contact the community owner's advertising team about placing an ad.

Cross-posting is posting the same message on several message threads. Cross-posting is also considered a breach of etiquette. Select a thread you believe has the right topic and best chance of garnering a response. If you don't receive an answer then consider moving on to another thread or starting your own. Many community members subscribe to several related threads and will notice multiple posts. If you're lucky, they'll call you out privately through a private message not in public in the thread – but don't count on it.

Forum software permits you to quote from another's post to help provide some context to your response. Don't quote the entire long message. You can delete those portions of the quote that don't apply in your response. Quote only the section that you are responding to.

Be careful with humor. Online RC communities are populated with folks from around the world. They may or may not understand your joke or may find it offensive. Same thing with slang. Your word may mean something entirely and embarrassingly different in another culture.

Use emoticons. Message tools usually have a selection of emoticons or 'smiley faces' you can add to your post to help communicate tone. Written messages can't communicate tone very well. It can be hard to determine whether someone is making a joke or is serious. By placing an emoticon in your message you can communicate tone better than words alone. You'll find emoticons for smiles, winks, embarrassment, frustration and others.

## YouTube

While not technically a forum-style online community, YouTube is a great online learning resource. You can use key word searches to zero in on the topic you need information on. As part of Google, YouTube's search results will display videos related to the topic searched on. Once you've selected a video to watch, other related videos will be displayed.

YouTube videos are a great way to see and hear about whatever it is you're interested in. In the RC arena, you'll find product reviews by both suppliers and end users. There are lots of videos on models showing both how they go together and how they fly once completed. You can find videos on how to attach CA hinges, how to program various computer transmitters and reviews on any number of RC gadgets and tools.

As with the online forums, content providers often enable YouTube's comments sections allowing you to post your response or questions about the video. Active providers will try to respond to comments and many times, others will respond, too. The volume of comments is nowhere near those in a traditional forum but content providers enjoy hearing from viewers and look forward to their 'like' counts going up. If you found the video helpful click on the 'like' icon.

Videos with ads attached are said to be monetized by the content provider. He or she will get a couple of pennies when ads are shown and especially when they are clicked on. If a relevant ad shows in a video, give it a click and help the content provider. Even user-produced videos cost time and money to develop. I have a couple of dozen videos on my YouTube channel. Search on my name and you'll find them. Most are video build logs on many of the models I've built as well as some flying videos of those same models plus others.

## Closing

Online communities should be one of your top choices when looking for answers to modeling questions. With the thousands of modelers who belong to these communities, someone is very likely to have the answer or an informed opinion on the topic you're interested in. By following threads devoted to the model you're flying, you can pick up on lots of hints and tricks to make flying your model more enjoyable.

Message threads are also very valuable resources when considering a new transmitter, model or other RC product. It's very likely that someone has already commented upon it and that others have added their opinions too. Modelers aren't shy about giving their opinions both good and bad about products they're using.

Online communities are a great source of knowledge for the new modeler. Take advantage of these great tools.

# Section Two

In this section we'll go a little deeper into how to operate your model. We'll discuss the basics of aircraft operations, motor and battery safety, finding a place to fly and basic club field operations.

# 7 Operating Your Model

Your success as a new model pilot will be based on how well you master some of the basics of model aircraft operations. This includes things like assembling your model, how to operate it safely and where it is safe to operate it. We'll take a look at these things and others in this chapter.

## Know your aircraft

Knowing your aircraft's quirks and components is a very important part of flying it successfully. Just like a full scale pilot is heavily schooled in his or her airplane's parts and performance, the successful model pilot should be too. If you have assembled a built up ARF with its balsa and ply construction and film covering, you probably have a good sense of how the plane is made. That may not be the case if the plane was a gift or a hand-me-down. Foam models don't have a lot of construction secrets you need to be aware of. Their parts are basically molded foam. Even these models, though, can have a few hidden surprises. Let's take a look at several important things you'll need to check prior to flight.

If you have been carefully following the instructions that came with your model, you should be in pretty good shape. Most models, when assembled per the manufacturer's instructions are going to be set pretty close to flight parameters. There are a couple of things worthy of double checking, though.

## Flight control security

Balsa and film models often come with their control surfaces attached to the primary structure with what are called CA-type hinges. These hinges are made from a stiff, thin, fabric. They are inserted into slots in the balsa structure and secured by dropping thin CA adhesive onto the fabric. The CA wicks into the slots following the fabric. When dry, the hinges are firmly bonded to the structure. A mistake new pilots often make is not checking the security of these hinges. Many times manufactures insert the hinges but don't glue them in. This allows the pilot to use other hinge types should they choose. It is not uncommon to have a new pilot bring their new plane out to fly only to discover the hinges aren't attached. Make sure your control surfaces are securely mounted.

Foam models usually attach control surfaces by molding them into the main structure such as the wing or horizontal stabilizer. The mold compresses the foam so the two parts are connected by a thin piece of the foam. These hinges usually work fine. Your model's instructions will normally advise you to flex the control surface numerous times before attaching the control rods. This loosens the foam providing less friction for the servo to overcome.

The down side to these molded hinges is that they can dry out and tear. The foam along the hinge line is very thin. If the control surface is bumped or twisted the hinge can tear loose. It can also just give up and separate after numerous of flights. Checking your hinges should be part of your normal preflight inspection. Molded foam hinges can be replaced with nylon hinges available at hobby retailers. You can also repair torn foam hinges using surgical tape such as Blenderm brand tape placed along the hinge line.

## Flight control adjustment

With the flight controls properly attached, you'll want to verify control deflection and direction. Many experienced pilots have crashed their models when the excitement of testing a new airplane caused them to overlook proper control movement and deflection.

There are a number of ways to attach the control rods that move the control surfaces. Follow the instructions that came with your model. Z-bends at the end of wire pushrods are easy to connect. Such connections are normally used on small, fairly slow flying models. For larger, faster models, manufacturers often use clevises where a pin is inserted through the hole in the control horn and snapped into the opposite side of the clevis. Modelers often use a sleeve of fuel tubing 4 to 5 millimeters wide or a small cable tie to secure the clevis. This prevents vibrations from causing the clevis pin to disconnect from the control horn.

Once connected, you'll want to ensure the control surfaces are centered or aligned with the primary structure they're attached to. To do this, you'll need to have your transmitter and receiver bound together if using a 2.4 GHz radio or simply matched to the right channel if using a 72 MHz system. With the trims centered on your radio, apply power to your model. Adjust the control surface until it is aligned. This is done either by sliding the push rod through an 'EZ' connector or by twisting the clevis on its threaded rod to lengthen or shorten it as required. Do that with each control surface. Either disconnect the motor from the ESC or remove the propeller before applying power to the model. The chance of you bumping the throttle control or knocking the radio over when adjusting the control surfaces is very high. Be safe. Having your model chase you around the workshop sounds funny but is extremely dangerous.

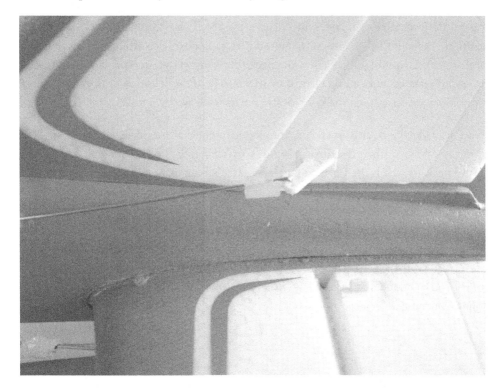

Figure 7.1. Small plastic clevis on flight control. Note fuel tubing slid over for security.

When you're happy the control surfaces are properly aligned, it is time to check for proper movement. We'll discuss basic aerodynamics in Chapter 11 so we'll limit the discussion here to say that ailerons should move opposite to each other and the 'up' aileron should be on the side to which you want to turn. Back stick on the right stick (mode 2) should command an upward movement for the nose. That means the elevator should move up when the stick is moved toward the bottom of the transmitter case. The reverse should happen when the stick is moved toward the top of the transmitter case. Rudder and steering should match the rudder control stick's movement.

If the controls move opposite to the desired direction, you will need to reverse the servo direction on your transmitter. On a basic transmitter you'll find small recessed switches labeled for each control channel. Move the switch to the other position and recheck the control surface's movement. If you have a computer radio, you'll need to move to the servo direction programming screen and reverse the selection. Again, check the movement after making the change. Unfortunately, transmitter brands don't agree on what full throttle is. As a result, depending on your transmitter's brand, full throttle could be commanded with the stick in the full down position requiring a servo reversal on the throttle channel, too. This is another reason to make sure the propeller is off when powering up your model for the first time.

Control deflection also includes the degree to which the control moves, not just the direction. Your model's instruction should include a chart describing the distance each control surface should move. You can check this using either an especially designed tool with a curved ruler with spring clamps to attach to your model or you can get pretty close just holding a ruler against the control surface to see how far it moves.

If you discover the control surface is moving too much or too little, you can change the geometry of the push rod's throw. Do this by changing the hole in the servo arm or control horn to which the push rod attaches. It is all about the radius of the arc and the corresponding movement. For example, the push rod will move a greater distance when placed in the outside hole of the servo arm for a given number of degrees of rotation at the servo's center as compared to a rod attached to a hole closer to the rotation point. At the control surface side, 5mm of push rod movement when attached to the outside hole of the control horn will cause less deflection than 5mm of movement when the control rod is attached to the inside hole. It is normally better to have the push rods mounted in similarly spaced holes.

Figure 7.2. Flight control deflection meter.

In other words, rather than change one end of a control rod from the inside hole to the outside hole to get your desired deflection, change both ends to middle holes.

If you have a computer radio, you can then fine tune the control surface deflection using sub-trim settings or adjusting servo end points. Read about them in your radio's manual.

## Center of Gravity

The last set-up item we need to discuss is the center of gravity or CG. Your model's instructions will likely have a chart marking the model's desired center of gravity. It is normally marked using a circle divided into quarters with the opposite quarters darkened. There will also be language describing the desired location. For example, the instructions may say, "the CG should be in a range of 70mm to 80mm aft of the wing's leading edge when measured at the wing's root."

The center of gravity is a point at which the entire model would balance if you could place it on the tip of a pen or pencil. The CG diagram in the instructions is focused on fore and aft balance. Marking the CG location on the model and placing it on a CG machine or on the tips of your index fingers at that point should result in the model balancing fore and aft.

If you are sure of the CG mark and the tail of the model drops, weight is needed in the nose. The reverse is also true. When balancing an electric model, be sure to mount whatever battery you plan to use when measuring the CG. The battery represents a significant weight. In many electric models, moving the battery a bit forward or aft will be all it takes to get the CG perfect. If you plan on using more than one size battery, balance the model using each battery and annotate their proper location in the fuselage using a marker. If you are balancing a low wing model, measure the CG with the model upside down. The fuselage should hang below the balance point on the wing.

Proper CG is critical to a good first flight. An airplane that is a bit nose heavy is OK. One that is tail heavy will be difficult to control. There is an old saying about CG, "A nose heavy airplane won't fly well. A tail heavy airplane won't fly long." Make sure you've got your CG set correctly.

You should also check your model's lateral CG. This is done by lifting the model from the tip of the propeller spinner and the lower trailing edge of the rudder. If the model rolls left or right it is out of balance. Check to see what might be causing that roll. Different sized servos for the ailerons or all the electronics mounted on one side of the fuselage are possible reasons. Lateral balance problems can often be fixed by simply mounting a small screw into the wingtip. Attach it with tape while figuring out how big a screw to use. Once you've found the screw that balances the airplane, screw it in. Remember, a small amount of weight further from the CG can make a big difference.

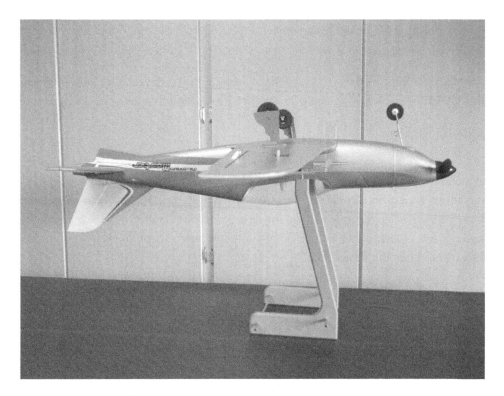

Figure 7.3. An aircraft balanced on a CG machine.

Setting up and double and triple checking your model is time well spent. Ensuring things work the way you want and that parts align properly will result in a maiden flight where only small adjustments are needed. It is not unusual for popular models that have been carefully set up to require only a click or two of trim to fly perfectly. On the other hand, that same model with flight controls out of alignment or deflections miss-set can be a real handful once airborne.

## Know your radio

Radio control transmitters can be pretty easy or highly complex. Knowing the capability of your radio is important to your ultimate success. Here are a couple of things you should be aware of.

## Basic Radios

A basic radio transmitter will have mechanical switches for its functions. You will need to know whether your radio is Mode 1 or 2 so you'll know what stick movement moves each control surface. You'll also notice control surface trim buttons alongside each stick. These switches may actually rotate with a tactile 'click' either up and down or left and right depending on the stick direction or they may add trim a click at a time by moving the trim button one way or the other while the button always returns to the centered position. Centering the trim when the button rotates is much easier than centering trim when the button always returns to center.

Your basic radio transmitter will also have those recessed switches referred to above. They are used to reverse the servos' direction. That grouping of switches will often include a mix switch to configure the radio for a model with elevons. In this case, the left and right signals are mixed with the up and down signals since there are not separate elevators and ailerons.

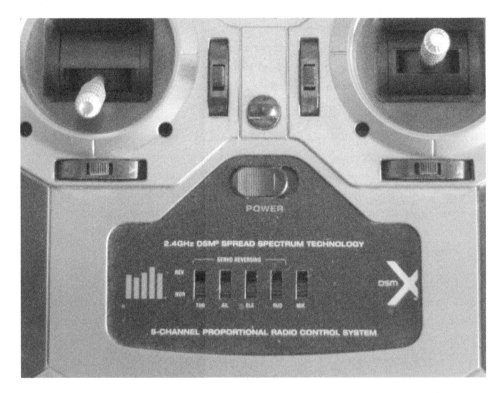

Figure 7.4. Servo reversing switches on a basic transmitter.

Your basic transmitter may also include flap and gear switches along with a trainer switch. All transmitters will obviously include a power switch. Read the manual or instruction sheet that comes with your particular transmitter to familiarize yourself with what each switch does and practice handling the radio so you can manipulate trim, gear and flap controls without looking away from your model.

## Computer Radios

As mentioned before, a computerized radio control transmitter is a very complicated piece of equipment. Working through the various options and variables to get your model ready to fly could very likely be a time consuming process for the first few models you program into your transmitter. As with the basic radio transmitter, you'll want to be thoroughly familiar with the dials and switches on your radio and be able to manipulate them while looking at your model.

Unlike the basic radio, your computer radio will likely have trim buttons that return to center when actuated. Fortunately, your computer transmitter's LCD screen will display the degree to which each channel's trim is offset. You'll be able to just hold the trim button in the direction you desire and watch the display move toward the centered position when setting up you model.

Also unlike the basic radio, your computer radio will reverse servo direction using options in the programming menu instead of physical switches. While the result is the same, the adjustment process is different.

Many computer radios allow you to select which switch controls which function. Obviously the power switch, flight control sticks and trim buttons aren't going to change but others can. For example, you will often be able to assign flaps to a two or three position switch or to a slider switch. If you have a 7 to 10 channel radio (or more) discuss switch assignments with an experienced modeler. You wouldn't want to have to remember what switch controls what depending on the model. Develop a switch assignment scheme and try to stick to it so you don't confuse functions when moving from plane to plane.

Programming your computer radio differs greatly from brand to brand. While the functions and selections will be the same, how you navigate to that selection or what that selection is called can vary. You will need to reserve some time with your owner's manual and radio to get the most from your transmitter investment. You may want to review Chapter 2 for additional information on computer radio transmitters.

## Closing

There's a lot to check before your first flight. Double and triple checking can make the difference between a great success and a disappointing disaster. It's a good idea to make a list of things you want to check. Make some notes as you go through your model's and transmitter's instructions.

# 8 Model Safety

Your model will bring you a lot of fun and enjoyment. For that to happen consistently, you'll need to develop safety habits that limit your chance of being injured by your model. Unfortunately, models aren't just bigger toys for bigger boys (and girls). They are complex machines that can cause serious injuries and damage if not handled properly. We've already referred to some safety practices. We'll double down on those and add others in this chapter.

## Motor Safety

Your model's motor and propeller present the greatest threat of personal injury. Unlike glow powered internal combustion engines on some models, electric motors can and will start any time they get power. A glow powered plane will have to be started by going through a start sequence. The pilot knows when the motor is started since he or she started it and due to the noise. Your electric motor is different.

The motor in your electric powered model has the capability to start anytime the throttle is moved out of the off position and the battery is plugged in. Newer electronic speed controls (ESCs) will not activate if the throttle is not at off when power is applied. However, once the throttle is placed to off, the ESC will activate. This means that if the throttle is then moved out of the off position the motor will spin. Some new transmitters also have a motor activation switch. The motor will not spin until the battery is plugged in and the ESC activates and the switch is moved out of the safety position. These new electronic features are great at helping limit injuries. They are, however, electronic safeties that can fail. Your best option is to remove the propeller from your model anytime you plan to make adjustments that require power to the model.

It is simply too easy to lose track of where the tail or wingtips are and move the model knocking over the transmitter. Such a fall will often result in the throttle being moved to full open and the motor springing to life. Since we're talking about electric motors, the motor won't stall and stop when it hits something. It will just bounce and keep spinning until the throttle is returned to off or the battery runs out of power. That means when the propeller hits something it will keep striking it again and again. If that something is your arm or hand, you will suffer serious injuries that could easily result in hospitalization.

If your radio has fallen to the floor or is on the opposite side of the work bench, getting to it can be difficult when trying to hold onto or stay out of the way of a model under full power. It only takes a couple of minutes to remove a propeller. With the motor at full power with no propeller, it's just noise.

It's also important to stay clear of the propeller when preparing to take off or when recovering your model. Most club facilities don't allow aircraft to be taxied to the runway. That means you'll be carrying your model. From the point where you are about to plug in the battery until after disconnecting it at the conclusion of your flight, always assume the propeller could start at any moment – completely without notice.

Lift your model while standing behind it and keep your arms, hands and body well away from the propeller arc. Think of your model the same way firearms instructors teach people to treat guns. Always assume it is loaded. With our electric models, always assume the propeller is armed. It's great if you have safety switches built into your transmitter. Use them! However, consider them to be the second or third line of defense, not the first. Remove propellers when working on your model and stay clear of them anytime your model is powered up.

Whether powering up your model for flight or maintenance, start by turning on the transmitter and selecting the right model. With the transmitter double checked that the throttle is off, then plug in the model's battery. The transmitter needs to be on first and off last.

## Battery Safety

Most electric models today use lithium polymer batteries to power their motors. We'll talk more about batteries in Chapter 14 of this book. For now, we'll just focus on some basic battery safety tips.

Lithium batteries are used to power all kinds of portable electronic devices today. If you have a smart phone in your pocket, you're probably carrying a lithium battery around with you. Lithium batteries need a bit more care than older alkaline batteries. The batteries in our models need even more care as they are usually much larger than the batteries in our phones.

Lithium batteries need to be charged with a charger made specifically for lithium batteries. Chargers made for nickel cadmium or nickel metal hydride batteries aren't programmed to determine when the lithium battery is fully charged. As a result, the battery could catch fire and explode. Chargers made especially for RC models will often allow you to set the kind of battery being charged and the amperage used to charge it. Be sure to use a charger or charger setting especially designed for lithium batteries. Use a charge rate appropriate for the battery being charged. Unlike other battery chemistries that are safe to leave on the charger overnight, you should always charge your lithium batteries on a fire proof surface or in a charging bag. Don't leave them unattended. My preferred method incudes using lipo bags and charging outside.

Lithium batteries need to be used within their limits. Motor and propeller combinations that pull more amperage than the battery can safely provide will damage the battery and can cause the battery to puff up like a marshmallow. In extreme cases, the battery can expand to the point where the case ruptures. When the chemicals inside the battery are exposed to air, they burn. Should your battery come back from a flight hot and puffed up, place it in a bucket of sand or on some other fireproof surface until it cools. Never put it into your vehicle while hot. Using the recommended motor/propeller combinations reduces the opportunity to over amp your battery. Use a watt meter when experimenting with different props. We'll talk more about watt meters in Chapter 18.

Crashes can also damage lithium batteries. In extreme cases, batteries can ignite after a crash if their cases are torn open or if the crash causes a direct short which causes the battery to overheat and rupture. More often, the battery's shrink wrap case is split and the battery cells show crush damage. Follow the battery manufacturer's instructions for disposing of the battery. Don't throw a partially charged lithium battery into the trash.

Transport your lithium batteries inside a fireproof container. Many modelers visit their local military surplus store and pick up a couple of metal ammo boxes for this purpose. Since these often seal tight, drilling a small hole in the lid to allow pressure to escape should a battery catch fire is a good idea.

Mishandling lithium batteries has caused damage to cars, workshops and homes. Read and follow the battery manufacturer's recommendations and you'll greatly reduce the chance of an accident or incident.

## Operational Safety

It is the pilot's responsibility to operate their model safely. You are liable for damage or injury to others. The best place to start on this topic is with the AMA's Safety Code. The AMA speaks for the modeling community and is recognized as an organization with deep experience and credibility in operating model aircraft. The AMA Safety Code is followed at all AMA club fields and AMA members pledge to abide by the code as part of being a member of the academy. You can easily find the most up-to-date version of the code on the AMA's website or by searching Google or Bing.

Whether you decide to join the AMA or not, following the AMA Safety Code is a good idea. Staying clear of full scale aircraft and not endangering people on the ground is pretty much common sense but there are a number of YouTube videos out there that seem to prove otherwise. Park flyers in particular face a more challenging task of staying away from people as spectators can insert themselves into unsafe areas and children can decide to kick balls or run through the overflight area without warning. This is much less of an issue at a club field. The club will have procedures to separate people and airborne models.

## Closing

Much of your enjoyment of the hobby will be based on your understanding of basic safety considerations. Work to develop good safety habits and make them part of your normal, day-to-day activities when working with your models.

# 9 Where to Fly

Finding a place to fly your model will be one of the first tasks you'll have to undertake. As describe in Chapter One, knowing where you will fly your model is one of the variables you'll need an answer to before selecting a model. Here are some places you may want to consider and some things to check on before assuming they are OK to use.

## Club Fields

We've already discussed club flying at some length. Choosing a club field will ensure you have an approved and fairly large area in which to fly. Clubs may have rules about the size of models flown or the methods used to power them. For example, some clubs are electric only due to noise restrictions at their location. Others may not allow turbine powered models for the same reason. Electric models are seldom impacted by power system rules.

Refer back to Chapter 4 to refresh your memory about things to consider when choosing a club. A local club with a dedicated flying site that fits your personality is often the best choice when choosing a flying site.

## Parks

City or town parks can also be a good choice for a flying site. With the growth of small electric models the term 'park flyer' was coined to refer to pilots who use these spaces. Parks present a couple of challenges, however. Since parks are open to the community, you'll likely find others enjoying the park, too. Flying your model will require much more space than a picnic so claiming a bunch of space and trying to keep others out will be difficult. Remember overflying people, structures and vehicles is contrary to the AMA Safety Code so you'll be at the mercy of others using the park.

Figure 9.1. A well-kept club flying site with a crushed granite runway.

Cities and towns may also have ordinances prohibiting model flying. Old ordinances normally envision large, heavy models with glow engines. You may be able to find a loop hole for small electric models or get the governing agency to change the rules. It's worthwhile to get clarification from the park manager. Getting it in writing or with a reference to an ordinance or rule might also be helpful if law enforcement asks you to leave. I don't recommend challenging a police officer, but having the rule allowing your action handy might be helpful.

## School Facilities

School facilities present the same opportunities and challenges that parks do. Since schools are usually managed by a different legal entity such as the local school board, the rules may be different from your local park. Where I live, school playgrounds are locked. Sports teams are given access but neighbors aren't allowed in whenever they want. Such limitations are often due to liability concerns. If you have easy access to school property, it's in your best interest to inquire about using the space. Large practice fields or empty baseball fields might be great for your needs. Check first.

## Private Property

Depending on where you live, there may be large open areas to fly. Someone or some entity owns that property. Getting permission from your neighbor, business owner or a nearby farmer could be an easy way to enjoy a wide open flying area. Again, it is in your best interest to find out who owns the land and ask for permission to fly there. The liability insurance you have through your AMA membership may help you when making your request.

## Operating Safely

Regardless where you ultimately choose to fly, operating safely is your primary goal. Then comes having fun. One of the best ways to have your permission to use a flying site revoked is to allow unsafe operations that threaten to damage property or injure people. Actually damaging property or having paramedics show up to treat injuries is even worse.

Club sites have insurance agreements in place and the land lord has an expectation of an occasional minor incident. Park supervisors, the principal of your local school or business owners are not likely to be so forgiving. They will be worried about their liability should accidents occur. If they have been willing to give you or your small group of flyers a chance, you need to be extra vigilant in enforcing safety rules.

Things such as flying behind other pilots, buzzing passersby or flying too close to the folks playing ball are things all pilots at the site should avoid. If it is an open space used by pilots from around the community, the person who has sought permission should make sure others know the limits and that all users help enforce safe operations. It only takes one foolish operator to cause your property owner or manager to withdraw permission to use their space.

Flying model aircraft is one of those hobbies that requires space to enjoy. If you choose to fly at other than flying club facilities, take the time to do your homework to identify safe places with a willing land owner. Making inquiries and establishing a relationship with the owner is a much better starting point than seeking permission after they have called law enforcement about your trespassing or violating a local ordinance. Presenting yourself as a responsible, respectful hobbyist can get your negotiations off on the right foot.

## How much space?

The amount of space you're going to need to safely operate your model will depend on several factors. Let's take a look at a couple of the important ones.

## Plane size

Your model's size is the primary factor you'll need to consider when finding a place to fly. How you plan to fly the model is a close second.

Most airplanes that fall into the park flyer category can be flown in the space equivalent to a little league ball field. Whether it is an actual field or an equivalent space in a park doesn't matter. Larger planes fly faster and will need more space. Fast planes, regardless of size will need more space. Flying in a tight circle all the time gets boring but that is what you'll end up doing if your plane is too fast for the space you've chosen.

On the other hand, if you primarily fly or plan to fly 3D-type maneuvers, you'll be able to get by with much less space. Spins, hovers and tight loops don't take much room. That is not to say you should try to fly your 80-inch 3D plane on a ball field but a 45-inch Parkzone Visionaire or Multiplex Acromaster would work just fine.

For trainer planes, a school playground or ball field will require one of the smaller trainers. Something like the Parkzone T-28 Trojan or Hobbyzone Super Cub S can be flown within that space though you'll be turning frequently.

Larger planes such as the E-flite Apprentice and other trainers with 60-inch wingspans or more will require space equivalent to a club field. That might be an actual club field or yours or your neighbor's pasture. Having 20 - 40 acres of available overflight area will give you enough room to enjoy your model without being too constrained. In describing guidelines for club flying facilities, the AMA recommends an area 1500 feet horizontally on either side of the pilot or 3000 feet from left to right. It also recommends 500 feet of space in front of the pilot. When you do the math this equates to 1,500,000 square feet or 34.4 acres. As you can see, medium to large sized models take a lot of space to operate safely.

Depending on where you live, trees may be a factor in your space planning. A couple of trees in your overflight area should not be a big problem. However, lots of trees along the edges of your flight area or close to where you plan to take off and land can be problematic. More than a couple of models have spent weeks stuck in a tree until the wind blew them down.

## Runways

A runway of some kind may or may not be required. Many small trainers can be hand launched. For those glider-like models with the motor on the top of the fuselage facing rearward, a hand launch and belly landing is the normal mode of operation. For small trainers with landing gear, landings don't take the distance that takeoffs do so only a small clear area is required. Don't plan on catching flying models. Doing so is contrary to the AMA Safety Code and as should be obvious – it's very dangerous.

Runways can take several forms. In many cases, the runway is simply a strip of dirt graded smooth. In other cases, they are grass-covered but mowed fairly short. Large, established model clubs often have asphalt runways up to 75 feet wide and 500 to 800 feet long. For small planes with small wheels, hard surface or dirt runways are best. Grass can sometimes catch small wheels and flip the plane over. The dirt infield of a baseball diamond works well for small trainer aircraft.

Inventive modelers have developed a variety of runway materials. Basically a strip of anything that can be spread over a fairly smooth surface can be used. Heavy plastic sheeting can be nailed to the ground to form a smoother surface for small wheels to navigate. There are also specialty fabrics made for this purpose. Finely crushed granite is also used to form a fairly hard surface for model operations.

Your space may also have a side walk or parking lot placed at a helpful location. Sidewalks can be difficult to land on due to their size but they can easily be used for the short takeoff rolls of small trainer aircraft. Grass landings with small trainers work well. Even if the model flips, you shouldn't expect any damage. Parking lots present two issues. One is cars. Remember you don't want to overfly vehicles. The other is light poles. A collision with a pole will cause major damage to your model. When focused on flying the model, many pilots lose track of these obstacles. That big silver pole is much easier to hit than you'd think. If using a parking lot to take off from, consider using the space next to the lot for your overflight area. Again, this assumes you have permission to fly there.

## Overflight area

Club flying sites may include the land under the overflight area in the terms of their lease or property agreement. In other cases, the club's parking, aircraft preparation area and runway may be all they lease or own. The area over which they fly may be used under an additional agreement with the land owner. For example, one club I'm aware of has a lease with the forest service for their primary site with a letter of understanding regarding overflight of land outside the club boundaries. The same thing may occur in rural areas where the club may lease a small patch of land for a runway and pit area and use the rest of the farmer's field or pasture as overflight area under the agreement.

Agreements with park departments and schools should be clear about what areas can be overflown. As discussed already, AMA rules prohibit flying over unprotected people, structures, vessels and vehicles. Be sure to consider the overflight area when choosing your space or when choosing a model for the space you've secured.

There are lots of YouTube videos depicting pilots flying over their neighborhoods. These flights violate the AMA Safety Code in that the model is flying over both unprotected people and structures. While the quiet street in front of your house might seem like a good runway, you must also consider the overflight area.

## Closing

Since this is a book directed at beginners, you should assume you'll need more rather than less space. It is going to take some time and practice for your mind to translate the visuals from your eyes into control movements on your transmitter. During that time your model is still moving. It is not unusual for a new pilot to get the model out near the edge of the flying area and get confused about what needs to happen to get it back. While he or she is making up their mind the model is moving even further away.

If you are particularly space challenged, all is not lost. Consider choosing one of the micro-sized trainers with advanced electronics. Those can be easily flown in a small park or ball field. The advanced stabilization features will allow them to deal with a bit of a breeze and to perform more like a larger model while requiring much less space. When space is an issue, bigger is not better when it comes to model selection.

# 10 Field Operations

Much of what is discussed in this chapter is directed at those pilots flying at a club setting. However, some of the topics have applicability to flying in non-club settings, too. The issue for non-club settings is that there is likely no overriding group or individual who can enforce common practices. If you are flying in such a setting, following these suggestions will identify you as a responsible flyer and safe operator.

## Pit Area Safety

The pit area is that part of the flying site where modelers assemble and prepare their models for flight. Established clubs may have shade structures and tables permanently mounted and available. In other cases, the pit area is simply that area reserved for members to erect pop-up canopies and folding tables to prepare their models.

Most clubs do not allow internal combustion engines to be run in the pits. The close proximity of other modelers makes running airplane engines too dangerous, even with props removed. Similarly, most clubs do not allow electric airplanes to be powered up or 'armed' in the pit area. This means that your electric airplane should never have the battery that powers the motor plugged in while the model is in the pit area. Some clubs may allow the battery to be plugged in if there is an arming plug that physically breaks the circuit to the motor.

An armed aircraft in the pit area is an accident just waiting to happen. Even when the ESC or throttle cutoff switch on the transmitter is supposed to prevent motor rotation, there remains a chance that the motor will start unexpectedly. Since pit areas are often congested, you risk not only injuring yourself or damaging your model, you also put others' safety and models at risk.

The way this often happens is that the model is armed 'just to check something.' When armed the model is moved, the tail bumps the transmitter and knocks it off the table.

The fall results in the throttle moving to full open and the model's motor starts to rotate at full power. The model jumps off the table and into the model next to it or into the legs of the modeler standing with his or her back to it. Serious injuries occur. Unfortunately, this scenario is not a fairy tale. It happens all too frequently.

Simply put – do not arm or run models in the pit area.

## Safety Lines

There are several safety lines in most club settings. One is sometimes called the pit line or start line. This line is between the pit area and the runway close to the pits. This line marks the beginning of the area where aircraft engines can be started and run or electric aircraft can be armed. There are often tables set up just beyond this line to make starting and arming easier.

Some fields will also have a pilot line. This line marks the closest point the pilot can come to the runway. This setback is used to provide a safety buffer from pilots and aircraft on the runway. It is often marked with a low fence.

The edge of the runway closest to the pilots and pits is the baseline or safety line. This line marks the near edge of the flying area. Many single runway clubs define this line as one that goes beyond the runway to the edge of their flying area. No aircraft should be intentionally flown behind that line toward the pilot line. This line forms the base for all other measurements when establishing other limiting lines.

The last common safety line most clubs define is called the spectator line. As you probably guessed, this line marks the closest point spectators can approach the runway. In many cases, the spectator line will be marked by a four to six foot fence. The AMA recommends that the spectator line be at least 65 feet from the baseline that marks the near edge of the runway.

## Observers or Spotters

Observers or spotters provide an extra set of eyes to assist in safe flight operations. You should use a spotter anytime you plan on flying your aircraft above about 400 feet. In this case, the spotter's primary role is to be on the lookout for full scale aircraft. You must yield to full scale aircraft and remain well clear of them. Your spotter will help you do that.

Below 400 feet and at busy club flying sites, the spotter's role changes slightly. While looking out for full scale aircraft remains a responsibility, you wouldn't anticipate full scale aircraft at such a low altitude. In this situation, your spotter's role is to help keep you aware of other models in the area. Your spotter can direct you to climb or descend to avoid another model preventing a mid-air collision. He or she can also help maintain situational awareness around the runway. They can pull you out of the way of a model whose landing has gone bad or tell you to duck down if an overflight of your pilot station appears imminent. They can also confirm flight time limits on your timer and confirm the runway is clear as you approach to land.

One mistake spotters often make is they spend most of their time watching the pilot's model for whom they are spotting. With two of you watching your model you still don't have anyone clearing the area around you. A good spotter will be busy keeping an eye on other airborne planes and their potential threat to your model while keeping you informed. Your spotter should be your personal safety officer during your flight.

Observers or spotters are not required except under certain circumstances. Having one during busy times is, however, a good idea. As a spotter I've helped pilots avoid collisions and once pulled my pilot down to a crouch as an errant model flew close overhead. As a pilot, the only mid-air collision I've suffered was with only two airborne models and, of course, no spotters. Tag teaming spotter duties with a couple of flying buddies is a great way to add that social component to the hobby. You can share insights, ideas and recommendations. If your spotter is also a model pilot, you can also hand off your transmitter to him or her after that bug flies into your eye!

## Direction of Flight

Many club fields have an arrow or other indicator showing what direction the flight pattern is going. Most of the time, the takeoff and landing direction will be determined by the wind direction. Normally you'll want to take off and land into the wind. In so doing, your speed over the ground is lower by the amount of the headwind component of the wind speed.

When taking off with the wind, your aircraft will need to generate enough speed to match the wind speed before even starting to generate enough speed to take off. The result is an extra-long takeoff roll and potentially low climb angle.

When the wind is very light and variable or at a 90 degree angle to the runway, pilot preference or other considerations may determine takeoff and landing direction. Examples of such considerations might be things like a fence at one end of the runway that has to be cleared or a slope to the runway that makes going one way or the other a better choice.

## Box Patterns

In full scale aviation, the traffic pattern flown around the runway is often referred to as a box pattern. This is because the ground track over which the airplanes fly forms a rectangular box with one corner clipped off at an angle.

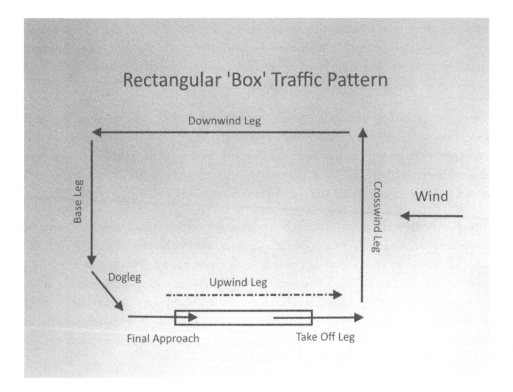

Figure 10.1. The rectangular 'box' pattern.

The four sides of this box have special names. The short leg flown 90 degrees to the runway after takeoff is called the crosswind leg. Since takeoffs are normally made into the wind, this leg is flown with the wind to the side of the aircraft. The leg parallel to the runway but opposite to the takeoff direction is called the downwind leg. It is so named because the aircraft is flying with the wind or with the wind on its tail.

The aircraft is said to be on base leg when the aircraft turns 90 degrees toward the extended center line of the runway when maneuvering to land. This leg is at the opposite side of the rectangular pattern as the crosswind leg. Oftentimes, it is easier to align the aircraft for landing by making two 45 degree turns than making one 90 degree turn. This cuts off one of the corners of the rectangular pattern. It is called dogleg, or dogleg to final as the ground track resembles a dog's back leg.

Once aligned with the runway, the aircraft is said to be on final or on final approach. If no landing is planned or after a touch-and-go practice landing, the aircraft is said to be on takeoff leg or on the upwind leg.

Traffic patterns where turns are made to the left are referred to as standard patterns. Left turns are preferred as they are toward the side that the pilot in command sits in most airplanes with side by side seating. That pilot has better visibility when turning left. Traffic patterns that demand right turns are referred to as non-standard patterns. In full scale aviation, a non-standard pattern might be used, depending on wind direction, when population density is higher on one side of the airport so all operations are restricted to the other side to reduce safety concerns or noise complaints.

Much of this terminology transfers directly into model aviation. Some clubs will specify pilots fly a box pattern to help ensure aircraft are going more or less the same direction in the same general area. That is not to say that there isn't space for turn reversals, aerobatics and other maneuvering, but on balance, aircraft near the runway should be heading the same direction that takeoffs are made and aircraft at the back of the flying area should be going more or less down wind. Take off and pattern direction is determined by the wind direction. At club flying sites, look for the arrow pointing in the traffic's direction.

When wind direction and velocity are not an issue, some pilots (me among them), advocate flying a box pattern where the takeoff leg is from the pilot's left to right. The aerodynamics of propeller driven aircraft tend to cause the aircraft to turn to the left on takeoff. With a left to right takeoff, that natural tendency will direct the aircraft way from other pilots and the pits. Just another safety factor to consider. Regardless, you should strive for proficiency in takeoffs and landings from either direction.

## Competition Patterns

You may find some of the pilots at a club site seem to spend most of their time just flying back and forth parallel to the runway. In many cases, you'll discover that they have spent a lot of time over the years practicing for and competing in aerobatic competitions. In these competitions they are required to complete a standard set of maneuvers very precisely. When these maneuvers are properly strung together, the result is a beautiful routine with various types of turn reversal maneuvers placed to keep the aircraft right in front of the pilot and the judges.

These patterns can be somewhat intimidating to other pilots more accustomed to a rectangular box pattern. This is because their models will often be nose-to-nose with the pattern pilot's model as he or she goes back and forth down the judging line. An easy way to deal with this potential conflict is to simply shift your box pattern further away staying out of the airspace right in front of you. Of course, you can simply wait until the pattern flyer finishes and enjoy the show.

## 3D and Free-for-All

Three D flying is when pilots use aircraft with lots of extra power that allows them to achieve extreme attitudes and do extreme maneuvers. Examples of this include hovering maneuvers, torque rolls and high alpha maneuvers. These maneuvers often result in the aircraft staying more or less in the same space for several seconds rather than moving around the pattern. Some of these 3D pilots will be practicing for contests built around this extreme maneuvering. As a result, the flow of the airspace is different. As with other competition patterns, as the new pilot flying around the box pattern, you can avoid these planes by shifting your flight pattern further out. 3D pilots generally like to be fairly close to their aircraft so they can see even the smallest movements and provide the appropriate input to their transmitter. If your flying site has a bunch of 3D activity, a spotter becomes an even more important asset to help you remain clear of other maneuvering models.

Figure 10.2. A large electric powered aircraft engaging in 3D maneuvering.

If you are flying in a park setting, you might find yourself in a free-for-all setting. These situations can remind you of the old World War I movie dogfights with airplanes going every which way. The bad news is that this environment increases your chance for a mid-air collision. The good news is that your lightweight foam park flyer will probably not be severely damaged.

## Runway Priority

When flying at a site with a runway, priority goes to the aircraft that is landing. If an aircraft has an emergency such as a stopped engine or has run out of battery power for the motor, those aircraft have priority over other landing aircraft. Getting a model safely back to earth is more important than a slight delay for a model waiting to take off.

To help manage runway operations pilots are expected to call out their intentions. For example, as you are about to enter the runway to take off, you should stop and visually clear final approach for other aircraft and then loudly announce, 'Taking off.' Then promptly enter the runway and start your takeoff roll. Pilots who anticipate landing are also expected to announce their intentions. Depending on how fast an airplane flies, the pilot should call out, 'landing' about the time they turn base. Use a loud voice so someone else doesn't attempt a takeoff in front of you. Announcing your landing when already on a short final is too late. It greatly increases the chance someone will taxi in front of you causing a go-around or worse – a collision.

When using a busy runway, it is polite to call out, 'clear' when your model has crossed the safety line. This allows other pilots to properly plan their landing or execute a go-around if they planned to land right behind you. This becomes more important when pilots aren't using spotters or observers who can tell them when the runway is clear.

Except for some preplanned or unusual situations, there should only be one aircraft on the runway at a time.

Occasionally, your airplane may come down in the overflight area or end up on its nose or upside down on the runway. It happens. As with announcing takeoffs and landings, be sure to loudly announce that you are entering the runway to retrieve your model. Pilots should carefully clear the final approach leg and then call out, 'On the runway.' This alerts others to the fact that they should not take off or land until the person is off the runway. Good practice is for the person who has been on the runway to loudly announce, 'Clear' when they return and cross the safety line.

## Closing

Nothing screams 'new guy' louder than someone who is unfamiliar with field operations and violates common safety and operational practices. Be sure to talk with other modelers to get a sense of what the rules are when flying at a club site for the first time. You should also take a look at any bulletin boards or signage that may have operating procedures spelled out. If you are flying with an instructor, be sure to have him or her quiz you on the proper actions you should take in various situations.

In a park setting, engage with others who are flying there. If there is a regular group who uses the area, it is likely that certain behaviors and procedures have been informally agreed to. Learn what they are and spend some time observing to see how they are practiced. Smoothly fitting in with others enjoying the hobby can add a valuable social component to your flying experience.

# Section Three

This section takes a deeper look into some of the important information you'll need to fully enjoy flying electric models. This will include some basic aerodynamics and a more detailed look at the components that make up your model's power system. We'll finish up with some suggestions on the tools and gadgets you'll need to complete your field box.

# 11 Basic Aerodynamics for RC Pilots

To get the most from your model flying, it's helpful to understand the various principles at work that allow your model to fly. Failure to understand some of these basic concepts can result in crashes and damage to your model. It's not unusual to see a pilot condemn their new model to the trash or give it away because, 'it's just a piece of junk,' when it is their knowledge about how an airplane flies that is the issue.

One can get advanced degrees in aerodynamics and things get very technical very fast. We're not going to go that deep. We are going to spend some time defining key concepts and pointing out some things you need to be aware of to get the most from your model. If you choose to go deeper there are some great resources available. For now it's just the basics.

## The Four Forces of Flight

Common explanations for flight start with explaining four forces that act on an airplane. Our discussion will be the same. The four forces acting on your airplane are lift, weight, thrust and drag. Lift acts opposite to weight and thrust acts opposite to drag. Getting the proportion of each correct allows the pilot to maneuver the aircraft.

## Lift

Simply defined, lift is a mechanical aerodynamic force produced by the motion of the airplane through the air. When lift is greater than weight, the airplane rises. When lift is less than weight, the airplane descends. The lift vector is represented by an arrow pointed perpendicular to the wings.

For the simple trainer airplanes you'll be starting off with, most of the lift your model produces will come from the wing.

Traditional explanations of lift usually include a discussion of what is called the Bernoulli Effect. Bernoulli was an 18th century scientist who studied fluids and what came to be known as fluid dynamics. Air is a fluid so his work applies to what we're talking about.

Among Bernoulli's discoveries is that as a fluid increases velocity, its pressure or potential energy decreases. We need to talk a little about airfoils before moving forward with Bernoulli and adding a bit of Sir Isaac Newton.

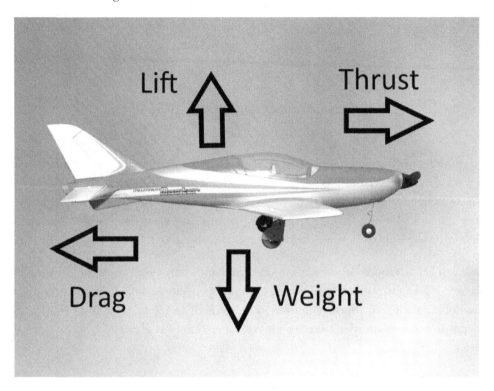

Figure 11.1 The Four Forces of Flight.

## Airfoils

Simply put, airfoils are curved surfaces specifically designed to achieve a desired ratio of lift over drag. On your trainer aircraft, the obvious airfoils are the wing, the horizontal stabilizer, the vertical stabilizer and the propeller blades.

Structures like wings have what is called camber. In this setting, camber is the degree to which the wing is asymmetric from top to bottom along a line drawn from the wing's leading edge to the trailing edge. This line is called the chord line. A typical trainer model's wing has a curve that has more distance to the top of the wing than to the bottom when measured from the chord. Such wings are called positively cambered wings. Wings where the distance from the chord to the top and bottom are equal are known as symmetrical wings. Small profile models with wings made from a flat piece of foam would fall into that category.

Recall that our definition of lift included the idea of movement through the air. Whether it is the propeller spinning on the motor shaft or the entire airplane cruising through the sky, we need air to flow over the airfoil to generate lift. Now back to Bernoulli.

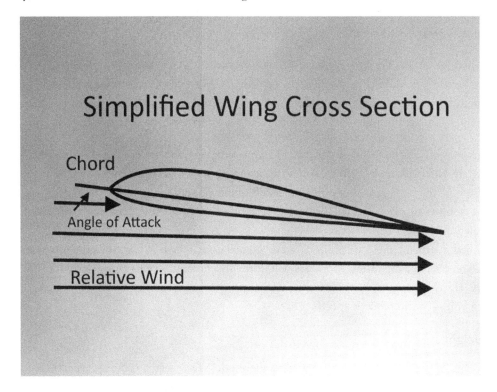

Figure 11.2. Simplified Wing Cross Section.

## Producing lift

Bernoulli's Principle is often applied to lift when dealing with positively cambered wings. You will often see explanations that say as the wing moves through the air the air on the top of the wing speeds up to cover the greater distance along the top surface of the wing to meet the corresponding airflow going under the wing. It is said that pressure differential causes the lower pressure on the top of the wing to pull the wing up or that the higher pressure on the bottom of the wing pushes the wing up. Unfortunately, researchers have shown the part about the air molecules rejoining at the training edge of the wing is false.

That is not to say that applying Bernoulli's Principle to a wing is wrong, just oversimplified. In fact, the flow over the top of a positively cambered wing is faster than the flow on the bottom and the lower pressure on the top side does contribute to lift. But there is more.

As the wing moves through the air it does so at an angle. The angle between the relative airflow and the wing's chord line is called the angle of attack. When the angle of attack is positive (when the extended chord line is above the relative airflow) some of the air that strikes the lower surface of the wing is directed downward. Think of a bank shot in billiards. Here is where Newton's Laws of Motion come in.

When the air hits the wing and is deflected downward, an equal upward force is imparted to the wing. Additionally, with the positive angle of attack, a low pressure area is formed behind the leading edge of the wing on the top surface. Air rushes downward to equalize the pressure. An upward force equal to the downward force is applied and lift occurs.

Given a specific airspeed, the higher the angle of attack, the greater the lift and the more the airplane will climb. Unfortunately, this can't go on forever. Depending on the specific shape of the wing, at some point the angle of attack gets too high and the airflow over the wing is disrupted to the point where little lift is produced. This angle of attack is called the critical angle of attack. When this angle is exceeded, the airplane is said to have stalled. As the plane stops producing lift you will notice the nose drops or the model may roll one way or the other. Modelers will normally encounter stalls at low speeds. That is not always the case. A stall occurs whenever the critical angle of attack is exceeded regardless of the model's speed.

## Weight

Weight is the force of gravity applied to the model. The weight vector is represented by an arrow pointed downward. The greater the aircraft's weight, the more lift it must produce to fly.

Modelers work to make their models as light as possible. Structures are made from light-weight balsa and light ply. Coverings, too, are light weight. One of the reasons foam models are so popular is that they weigh so little compared to models made from other materials. Modelers and manufacturers strive to include various components that are powerful enough to accomplish the task without the extra weight that goes along with larger components. For example, if an eight ounce capacity fuel tank will power a glow motor for the length of a typical training flight, why put in a tank that holds twice as much? The weight of the tank won't matter much but the weight of the extra fuel it holds certainly will. Same with things like servos. If a nine gram (torque) mini servo will do the job, why use a standard servo that both costs and weighs a lot more?

With electric powered models, you may have some choices regarding motors and battery sizes. Weight needs to be part of the decision. Larger motors may provide more power but they also weigh more. Larger batteries can often add many ounces to the overall weight of the plane. You will need to decide whether the extra flying time is worth it.

As the weight of the airplane grows, a factor called wing loading does too. Simply put, wing loading is the amount of lift each square inch (or other unit of measure) must produce for the airplane to fly. Aircraft with high wing loading must fly faster to produce the same amount of lift as a similarly heavy aircraft with low wing loading. Wing loading is adjusted by changing the airplane's weight or designing in a wing with more area. As a beginning modeler, you'll discover this when you add a supersized battery to your model and find the takeoff roll is longer and the model lands at a higher speed. The added weight adds to the wing loading requiring higher speeds to generate the necessary lift.

## Thrust

Thrust is the airplane's forward force provided by the propulsion system. In our models, it is normally provided by the motor through the spinning propeller. The thrust vector is depicted as an arrow facing forward from the nose of the airplane.

Thrust provides the speed or velocity the wings need to produce lift. Your almost-ready-to-fly or ready-to-fly model was designed and equipped to provide enough thrust to operate the model through its normal flight range. If you built your model from a kit, the instructions recommend a size or range of motor and prop sizes that will allow the model to perform well.

When thrust exceeds drag, the aircraft will either accelerate or climb. When thrust is less than drag, the aircraft will either decelerate or descend. Thrust is adjusted by moving the throttle control up or down. Advancing the throttle will cause the propeller to spin at a higher RPM. Reducing the throttle will have the opposite effect.

You can also adjust thrust by changing the propeller's diameter or pitch or both. The diameter is the length of the prop from tip to tip. It is the first number used when describing prop size. The second number in the prop's size description is its pitch. The pitch of the prop is the angle at which the propeller bites off the air. Smaller pitch propellers bite off smaller chunks of air than propellers with larger pitch. The pitch represents how far the propeller would move forward per revolution in a soft solid such as gelatin. A 9 X 6 propeller would have a diameter of 9 inches and a pitch of 6 inches. It would move 6 inches forward per revolution. A 9 X 6 propeller would produce more thrust than a 6 X 6 propeller spinning at the same RPM.

With an electric powered model, you can also increase thrust by increasing voltage. By moving from a 3-cell lithium polymer battery with a nominal voltage of 11.1 volts to a 4-cell battery with a voltage 14.8 volts, you'll be able to increase RPM and thus thrust. Both of these adjustments assume your power system can handle the additional loads. We'll discuss that more thoroughly in Chapter 17.

## Drag

The last of the four forces of flight is drag. Drag is the force that is opposed to thrust. For this high level discussion we'll divide drag into two categories – form drag and induced drag. The drag vector is depicted as an arrow pointed reward from the tail of the airplane.

Form drag is the resistance caused by the physical structure of the airplane moving through the air. It includes the friction caused by the air molecules rubbing against the airplane's skin and the impact of molecules against the leading edge of the wings and tail surfaces, nose, flying wires and other aircraft structure. Designers try to reduce form drag by adding smoothing structures such as fairings where the wings join the fuselage and other streamlining techniques. Modelers can reduce form drag by building models that aren't warped and flying them in coordinated flight. Models with dirty or bumpy surfaces also increase form drag.

Induced drag is the resistance caused by producing lift. The more lift being produced the greater the induced drag. You recall that a wing producing lift has a low pressure area on its top side. The higher pressure air on bottom side rotates from the bottom to the low pressure area on the top at the wing tip. This movement forms a vortex rotating inward from the wing tip toward the fuselage. This vortex extends rearward behind the aircraft. This vortex produces a rearward force that is applied to the airplane. Thus by producing lift, the wing induces (or creates) drag.

In full scale aviation, these vortices are very dangerous. The rotating air from a heavy jet can easily exceed a small plane's control authority causing the aircraft to roll within the vortex. This can cause crashes when low to the ground. It is also why there are spacing requirements between large and small aircraft for both takeoffs and landings.

You may also have looked at an airliner and seen the small upturned tips on their wings. These 'winglets' change the formation of the wingtip vortex and reduce induced drag. This drag reduction saves airlines lots of money on fuel costs.

## Balance – or not

As the pilot, it's your job to manipulate the relationship between these four forces to achieve the flight goals you desire. Straight and level, unaccelerated flight means all four forces are in balance. Lift equals weight and thrust equals drag.

As mentioned in the section on thrust, with more thrust than drag the aircraft will either accelerate or climb. With more drag than thrust, the aircraft must decelerate or descend.

When turning, the aircraft's lift vector starts to point sideways depending on how much bank the pilot commands. The vertical component of the lift vector shrinks meaning the weight vector increases in relation to it. You guessed it, the aircraft must start to descend. As the pilot, you must increase lift to match the weight vector to maintain level flight. You do that by adding up elevator. As the bank increases lift must also increase to maintain a level turn. Theoretically, you must achieve an infinite amount of lift at 90 degrees of bank.

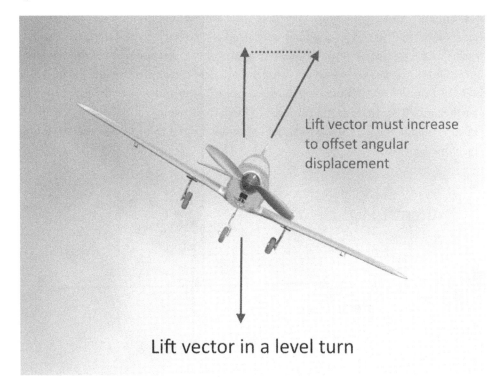

Lift vector must increase to offset angular displacement

Lift vector in a level turn

Figure 11.3. Lift vector in a level turn.

You will not be going through an ongoing mental conversation about all this each time you make an input to your airborne model. With practice these connections and need for balance will become second nature. It is important for you to understand what is happening, though. With a little background on the science, you'll be able to anticipate corrections and avoid situations that can be dangerous to your model. Now let's look at how you'll adjust these forces.

## Flight Controls

The airplane's flight controls are those components that allow the pilot to manipulate the four forces just discussed. We've learned that changing the relationship between lift, weight, thrust and drag is how you maneuver your model. Let's now take a look at each of the flight controls you will typically find on a trainer-style, radio controlled model. You'll find them on advanced models, too, of course, but we'll focus the discussion on trainers.

## Flight Axes

Since an airplane moves around in a three dimensional space, it has to be able to go up and down, left and right, and side to side. We'll describe these movements as rotations around one of three flight axes. The three axes are the longitudinal axis that stretches from nose to tail; the vertical axis that goes from top to bottom; and the lateral axis that stretches between the wingtips. In most diagrams these axes intersect in the fuselage at what would be the center of gravity – that point where the airplane would balance if you could set it on the tip of a pin or pyramid support. Your model has flight controls that cause the aircraft to rotate around an axis. In most maneuvers you'll be doing, you'll need to manipulate the flight controls together to get the desired results. Let's start by looking at each one separately.

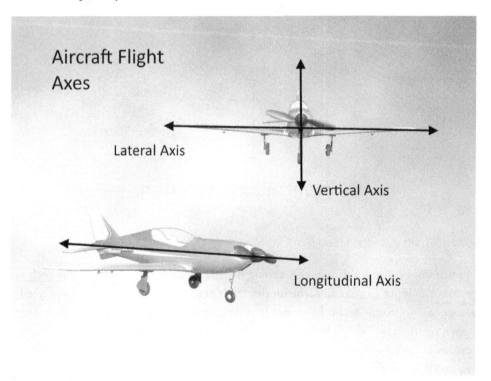

Figure 11.4. The flight axes.

## Throttle

The throttle probably isn't the first flight control most pilots think of when listing flight controls. However, throttle allows you to control your aircraft's speed. The power produced by the engine or motor is an important factor in achieving and maintaining the flight conditions you desire. For example, climbs require more power and descents require less. Your model's thrust curve may show that below a certain airspeed going even slower may require more rather than less thrust. That is where the saying about 'being behind the power curve' comes from.

## Rudder

The rudder is the moveable surface connected to your model's vertical stabilizer. The rudder rotates the aircraft around the vertical axis – that is, side to side. If your model was built true, it should fly straight through the air with no sideways tendencies. If not, a bit of rudder will help straighten the aircraft's path through the air. Deflecting the rudder to the left will cause the nose to move left and vice versa.

In most cases, you'll be using rudder to offset other aerodynamic forces during certain maneuvers. For example, most airplanes have a tendency to rotate left when power is applied during takeoff. You'll need to apply right rudder to offset this tendency. Once airborne, a phenomenon called adverse yaw occurs when ailerons are deflected. Again rudder will be used to offset that unwanted yaw. Keeping the airplane aligned is called maintaining coordinated flight. During turns, when the tail tracks inside or outside the turn radius it is called being in a slip or a skid respectively. Using the rudder properly avoids this.

Three channel models have wings that have significant dihedral or upward tilt and no ailerons. With these models, rudder provides the rolling movement needed to turn.

## Elevator

On conventional trainer models, the elevator is mounted at the trailing edge the horizontal stabilizer. The elevator rotates the aircraft around the lateral axis – that is, nose up and down. Pulling back or down on the radio transmitter's elevator control stick will cause the elevator to rotate up. This causes the aircraft's tail to go down and the nose to rise. When pushing the transmitter stick forward or up, the elevator rotates down causing the tail to rise and the nose to go down.

You will use the elevator in conjunction with throttle and ailerons throughout your flight. You'll add elevator and throttle together to climb and elevator in sequence with ailerons to roll into and out of turns. You will also manage total lift production using the elevator. As your model slows down, you will increase up elevator deflection to increase the wing's angle of attack. This will increase lift to maintain level flight at that new, slower speed. As discussed in the section on lift, you'll also increase lift (up elevator) during a turn to increase the lift vector that is now no longer vertical offsetting the weight vector.

## Ailerons

Ailerons are found on the wing's outboard trailing edge on most trainer aircraft. The ailerons rotate the aircraft around the longitudinal axis which stretches from nose to tail. Ailerons move opposite to one another. The aileron on the wing towards the turn direction moves up and the aileron on the wing away from the turn rotates down. This movement changes the lift produced by each wing causing the rotation around the axis.

Many people think that the ailerons are the flight control that turns the aircraft. As you've seen in the discussion on lift, that is not true. Ailerons simply direct the lift one way or another. By rolling the aircraft to the right, the lift vector now has a rightward pointing component. It is lift, as controlled by the elevator, which actually turns the aircraft.

On trainer aircraft with dihedral and fairly fat wings, the new pilot won't have to add a bunch of back stick to turn the airplane. Because it is a trainer, it's designed to be easy to learn on. Pilots are often surprised, however, when graduating to a more advanced model and they discover they have to add up elevator in turns. You may hear a modeler say that one particular model or another 'goes where you point it.' This statement often refers to the fact that the model won't turn unless elevator is applied.

## Flaps

Flaps are normally considered secondary flight controls. They are part of a group of controls on full scale aircraft that aid in controlling the aircraft across a wide range of speeds. Included in the group are trim tabs and spoilers. While it is certainly possible to see spoilers set up on a radio controlled model, especially a sail plane; trim tabs are seldom used.

Flaps are used to change the shape of the wing. By lowering flaps, the pilot changes the camber of the wing by changing the chord line. As you recall from the discussion on airfoils, the chord line is a line drawn from the leading edge of the wing to the trailing edge. When the flaps are lowered the relationship of the trailing edge and leading edge changes creating greater camber. A wing with greater camber can produce more lift at lower speeds. This allows the aircraft to land at slower speeds. Flaps also increase drag. This means that the aircraft will slow down when the flaps are deployed. As the model's pilot, you can use flaps to help you slow down and you should anticipate the need for additional power to overcome the additional drag once you've slowed to approach speed with the flaps extended.

In some full scale aircraft and some very complex model aircraft, extending the flaps can also increase the wing's surface area (fowler flaps). In most cases, however, flaps just change the wing's camber and increase drag.

## Closing

It is important to understand how each flight control impacts your model. In practice you will seldom manipulate only one flight control at a time. Moving one flight control almost always impacts some other aspect of your model's performance. We discussed a few of those things already such as needing more power in addition to elevator to climb and needing both rudder and elevator in addition to ailerons to complete a coordinated turn. Even something as simple as an aileron roll can require forward elevator input as the model approaches inverted to compensate for the positive camber of many wings.

# 12 Motor Basics

Small, powerful electric motors are one of the things that have driven the popularity of electric RC model airplanes. Over the past several years, improvements in technology and burgeoning popularity of small brushless motors have made them the motor of choice for almost every model aviation electric power system. Before joining the brushless motor parade, however, let's take a little detour and discuss brushed motor construction and use.

## Brushed motors

As electric model airplanes became more popular, they were primarily powered by small brushed motors. Brushed motors come in several sizes and are known by numbers such as Speed 350, Speed 400, Speed 480, Speed 600 and so on. Most of these motors were designed to run on voltages from 6 to about 9 volts. You can still see remnants of this sizing system as some manufacturers still label some of their brushless motors as '480 sized' and so on.

All electric motors generate both revolutions and torque. This is done by changing the electric field generated by the motor's windings. This electric field has magnetic properties which interact with the actual magnets that are part of the motor's construction.

You know from experience playing with magnets that the like magnetic poles repel each other and the opposite poles attract each other. The electric motor makes use of this principle by causing the magnetic field generated by the motor's windings to change from positive to negative just as the rotating core aligns with the actual magnets' opposite polarity. When changed, the fields now repel each other and the core rotates to the next alignment point where the polarity again changes.

The changes in polarity are caused by changing the direction of the current's flow through the windings. Two components help accomplish this. One is metal strips that rub against the rotating center shaft of the motor. These are called brushes. The other component is a split metal ring that is attached to the shaft between the shaft and the brushes. It is called the commutator. The brushes provide the current to the commutator which, as it rotates, mechanically causes the current flowing in the motor windings to reverse as the brushes contact the different halves of the split ring.

The amount of current flowing to the model will determine how fast the motor rotates. This is controlled by the electronic speed control. We will discuss those more fully in Chapter 13.

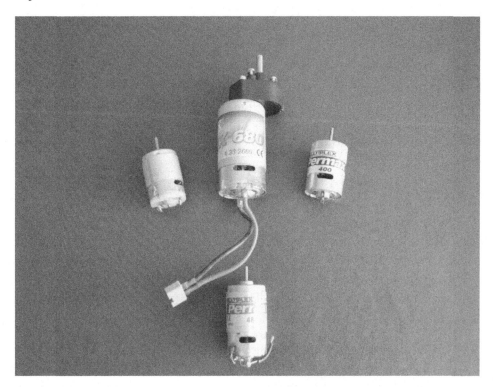

Figure 12.1. Speed 400, Speed 480 and Speed 680 brushed motors.

While these motors are fairly simple they have some drawbacks. For instance, the brushes rub against the commutator which causes friction that reduces motor efficiency. As the brushes wear, they become less efficient and they can even burn through causing motor failure. At a more technical level, as the motor rotates, the brushes span both sides of the commutator resulting in an instant of zero torque. Again, this reduces the motor's efficiency. Because the current reversals are handled mechanically, brushed motors are also electrically noisy. You will often see capacitors soldered to the outside of brushed motors in an effort to reduce electrical noise. This noise interferes with the receiver's ability to maintain connection to the transmitter – especially in the 72 MHz band. This is similar to what happens when listening to an AM radio station and you drive under high voltage transmission lines. The modeler can mitigate this by placing the receiver as far away from the motor as possible.

If you end up using a brushed motor for one of your models, consider breaking in the motor by running it at low speed for 15 to 20 minutes. The goal is to allow the brushes to slowly take on the curvature of the commutator. This results in more of the brush being in contact with the commutator extending brush life. If your motor came with break-in instructions, follow those.

Today you will find brushed motors mainly in small, foam models. Many of these will be older models that have been collecting dust on the shelf of your local hobby shop or available at a swap meet. Due to some of the other limitations to the power systems in these older electric models, many modelers will often upgrade the power system with more modern components in an otherwise nice airplane.

## Brushless motors

Brushless DC motors currently make up probably ninety-eight percent of the power plants for electric models. Their market growth since about 2010 has been extraordinary. This has been due in large part to the rapid reduction in price and the wide variety of sizes.

Earlier we mentioned that large brushed motors could take up to about 9 volts. Large brushless motors that can deal with over 40 volts are common. Some of these motors can generate over 2000 watts of power. That means giant scale models that just a couple of years ago would have only been glow or gasoline powered are now powered with electric power systems.

Instead of using a commutator and brushes to change the current flow and thus the magnetic polarity of the windings, brushless motors use an entirely different technique. As with the brushed motor, rotation is achieved by changing the polarity of the winding as an actual magnet approaches. How the polarity is changed is very different.

There are two kinds of brushless motors used in model aviation power systems. One is called an inrunner motor the other is called an outrunner motor. The components and how they work are the same but how they are constructed is a bit inside out.

Figure 12.2. Inrunner and outrunner brushless motors.

Both types of motors include wire windings wrapped around a form called a stator. These windings generate the magnetic field. Both motors also have rotors which include the magnets that interact with the windings' changing magnetic fields. Where they differ is inrunner motors have the windings on the outside with a motor shaft containing the magnets at the center of the motor. Outrunner motors are reversed. The outrunner has the stators and the windings in the center of the motor and the magnets with which the magnetic fields interact are glued to a bell or housing that spins on the outside. The motor shaft passes through the center of the motor and is normally connected to the bell with grub screws so when the bell rotates, so does the motor shaft.

Motors with more windings or 'turns' produce less revolutions per volt but more torque. This is called the motor's Kv rating. By changing the number of turns, manufacturers can produce motors to meet the modeler's specific needs. For example, when you know the size and weight and desired performance of your model (we'll discuss that in Chapter 17), you can choose a motor that will deliver power to meet that need. Small, fast models often use a motor with high revolutions per volt and small propellers that spin very fast. Larger models demand larger but slower spinning propellers. These large propellers bite off a big chunk of air so they need a motor with greater torque to be effective. Putting a large propeller on a high Kv motor would likely pull too many amps through the circuit and generate enough heat to damage or destroy the motor.

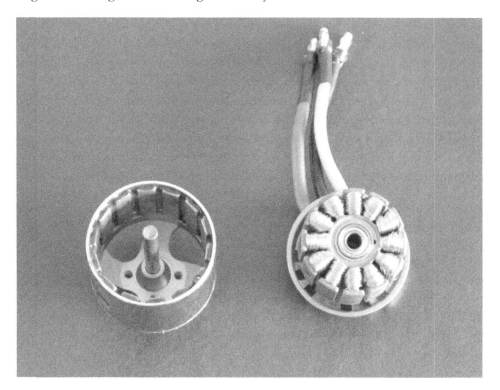

Figure 12.3. The windings and magnets of an outrunner motor.

Brushless motor windings are placed in groups of three. This allows the polarity to change causing even torque production throughout rotation. RC motors usually have several sets of these triplets to ensure even or constant operation as the magnets rotate. If you were to measure and chart the torque generated during the motor's rotation, you'd see that having multiple sets of winding triplets helps ensure a constant torque rating at each degree of rotation.

Motor manufacturers vary in how they label their electric motors. However, there seems to be two primary systems in the marketplace. In one system, the motor is described by a four digit number. The first two digits are the diameter of the stator on which the windings are placed. The second two digits are the length of the stator. Thus a 2814 brushless motor would have a stator 28 millimeter wide and 14 millimeters long.

Most manufactures then add the Kv rating for the motor. So staying with the previous example, you might be able to choose from a couple of motors such as 2814-1000Kv or a 2814-1400Kv depending on your power requirement. Knowing the stator width and length will give you a general idea of the motor's capacity as compared to another motor with different numbers. Generally, the larger the numbers the higher the capacity.

The second labeling system is newer and growing in popularity. In this system the label makes a comparison to an established motor or engine. For example, you will find small brushless electric motors labeled Power 480 or Park 450 or some other descriptor plus a number that represents an equivalent size of a small brushed motor. For larger motors you'll see a manufacturer's name or series letter and the equivalent glow engine displacement. For example, you might be looking at a Great Planes Rimfire 1.60 or a Turnigy G160. Both represent a motor with the approximate power of a glow engine with a 1.60 cubic inch displacement. In the case of the Rimfire 1.60, its label in the other labeling system would be 6362-250Kv so you could make some comparisons.

Just to make things even a bit more complicated, some manufactures will produce several motors using the same glow equivalent number but with varying Kv. This allows the modeler to further refine the motor choice to power their model.

Both inrunner and outrunner brushless motors are controlled by an electronic speed controller or ESC. We'll discuss them in more detail in Chapter 13. For now let's just say that the ESC uses electronic principles to detect where the motor is in the rotation cycle and changes the polarity of each set of windings to keep the motor spinning. Unlike brushed motors, because this commutation is determined electronically each brushless motor must have its own ESC.

## Inrunner Motors

Due to size limits, inrunner motors are normally used for high Kv applications. This could include powering an electric ducted fan (EDF) unit for a jet-style model or for spinning a small folding propeller on an electric powered sailplane. In older models, you may see an inrunner connected to a gearbox to slow the propeller's RPM and increase torque.

Inrunner motors are similar in size and shape to brushed motors. The obvious difference is there are three wires connected to the motor, not two. The ESC uses these wires to energize the windings in the sequence that causes the motor to rotate.

Since the rotor is in the center of the inrunner, the diameter of the stator and the actual diameter of the motor plus casing will be very close. Some inrunners will have heat sinks attached to help dissipate their operating heat so those motors' outside diameter will be larger. You'll need to be aware of the actual motor diameter when planning your installation. You may have a very narrow space in the model or the housing for your EDF unit may take a specific diameter motor and motor shaft. Double check to ensure everything will fit.

Over the last couple of years, inrunners have fallen out of favor. This is mainly due to the popularity of outrunner motors and their huge variety of sizes and Kv ratings. Nowadays, it is not unusual to see a small but very high Kv outrunner powering an EDF unit where in the past that job would have fallen to an inrunner.

## Outrunner Motors

Outrunner motors come in an amazing variety of sizes and capabilities. You can find micro outrunners as small as or smaller than 10 millimeters in diameter for indoor micro models. At the other extreme, large outrunners with 60+ millimeter diameters are available to power very large models with wingspans of greater than 100 inches. No wonder the outrunner motor rules the market in the electric airplane space.

Due to the spinning bell on an outrunner motor, the motor's dimensions will be larger than the width of the stator. When planning an outrunner installation or upgrade, it is important to know the actual width and length of the motor to ensure it will fit in the available space. If you are looking at an outrunner described using the stator width and length system, the actual motor will be considerably wider than the width number in the description.

An outrunner's motor shaft is connected to the rotating bell. The bell and shaft can be pulled from the motor windings by either removing a small 'c' clip or a couple of grub screws. You can, therefore, replace the motor shaft should a crash or nose-over on landing occur bending the shaft. Replacements are readily available for most motors. You may want to investigate replacement shaft availability when choosing a motor as part of your decision process.

Additionally, since the shaft can be removed it also can be moved or shifted. In some installations you'll want the outrunner's rotating bell behind the motor mount or firewall. In other cases, you'll want it out in front. By loosening the grub screws that hold the shaft to the bell, you'll be able to push the shaft through the end of the bell allowing the motor to be mounted either forward or backward. Shafts fit very tightly. Don't expect this to be a fingertip operation. In Figure 12.2, you can see the motor on the right has the shaft extending from the end opposite the bell. The other two outrunners have the shaft extending from the bell side.

With the huge variability and wide availability of brushless outrunners, it's important for you to look behind the top-level label and dig into the motor's other specifications. Spec sheets are usually available online and are often listed right on the motor's product page if you're ordering online. If you're at your local hobby shop, ask the clerk to open the box or pull a spec sheet from the file.

Similarly sized motors can have very different capacities. Be sure to look at and compare such things as voltage limits, amp or current limits, shaft diameter, wattage limits, Kv and overall weight. A slightly larger motor or the same size motor from a different manufacturer may suit your needs more exactly. Let's look at an example. The top level specifications for two motors from the same manufacturer are the same except for the Kv rating. Both are 3530 sized motors. One produces 1100 Kv the other, 1400 Kv. Looking below the surface, however, the 1400 Kv motor produces up to 180 more watts of power; can draw up to 9 more amps of current; costs $.10 more and weighs only .3 grams more. Those are big differences for small motors and could certainly influence your selection.

## Closing

Your motor selection will be one of the most important decisions impacting your model's performance. Spend a little extra time examining the variables we've discussed to ensure it can deliver the power you are anticipating.

# 13 Electronic Speed Control and Battery Eliminator Circuit Basics

Electronic Speed Controls (ESCs) and Battery Eliminator Circuits (BECs) are critical to flying electric aircraft. These two devices are often mounted on the same circuit board. They provide power to the motor and to the receiver. ESCs control the speed at which the motor rotates and BECs eliminate the need for an extra receiver battery and its associated weight.

ESCs for brushed motors work differently than ESCs for brushless motors so they cannot be interchanged. There are some differences in BEC construction, too. We'll discuss these critical components in this chapter.

## Brushed Motor ESCs

ESCs for brushed motors are pretty simple to understand. Since the commutation (current reversal) in a brushed motor is mechanical and occurs inside the motor, the ESC only needs to vary the current going to the motor. More current equals more speed. The ESC determines how much current to pass along to the motor by interpreting the signal from the receiver which reads your transmitter's throttle position.

The brushed ESC cycles the current to the motor on and off many times each second. When the throttle is closed the ESC switches the power off 100% of the time. When the throttle full open, the ESC switches the power on 100% of the time. Intermediate throttle positions result in a proportion or percentage of the time the switch is open or closed. A low throttle position results in the switch being open (no current) more than it is closed and vice versa for a high throttle setting. The motor sees this as a lower or higher overall current and reacts accordingly even though the full capacity of the battery is applied when the switch is closed.

Because the commutation is done mechanically inside the motor, you can use a single brushed ESC to power more than one brushed motor. That means you can use just one

ESC to control the motors of your B-17 model so long as the total current draw of all four motors is equal to or less than the amp rating for the ESC.

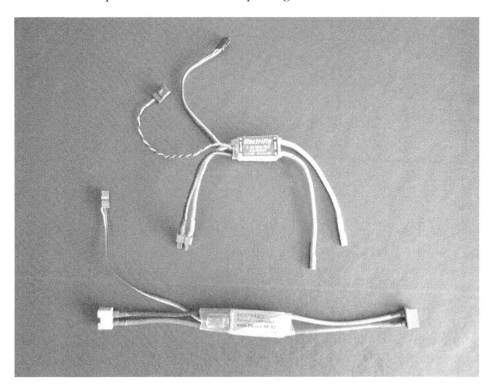

Figure 13.1. Brushed motor ESCs. Note the two wires going to the motor.

## Brushless Motor ESCs

ESCs for brushless DC motors are completely different from brushed motor ESCs. A brushless motor's ESC provides both speed control and commutation. This gets quite technical so we'll look at it from a fairly high level.

First let's discuss commutation. As you know from the chapter on brushless motors, the brushless motor has at its simplest form, three windings. How these windings are or are not energized determines the rotation of the motor. Most ESCs used in RC models determine the position of the rotor by estimating its position based on what is called Back Electromotive Force. The Free Dictionary defines this as "a voltage that occurs in an electric motor where there is relative motion between the armature of the motor and the external magnetic field." The ESC senses this voltage and uses it to indirectly determine the position of the rotor. Some brushless motors have sensors attached to them. Their ESCs use different electrical principles to determine rotor position. Our RC motors don't usually have such sensors and are referred to as sensorless motors. Now that the ESC knows the position of the rotor, it has to provide speed control.

Castle Creations, a developer of top quality speed controllers, describes power control to a brushless motor much the same as the voltage switching in a brushed motor ESC. They use a term called Pulse Width Modulation or PWM. The ESC breaks the power going to the motor into thousands of pulses per second. The proportion of on versus off power pulses determines how much power the motor sees. Using this technique designers are able to digitally simulate what would normally be an analog activity. In this case, that of using an analog rheostat to dial down the current going to the motor.

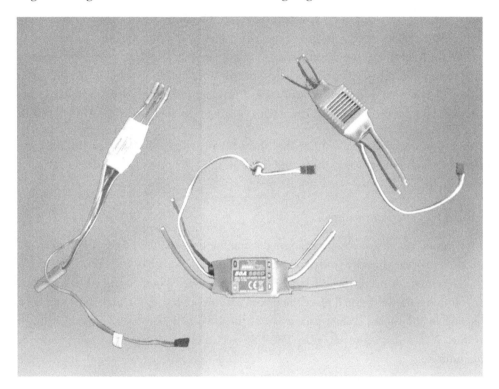

Figure 13.2. Brushless motor ESCs. Note the three wires going to the motor.

Since the current flowing though the circuit is 100% of what is available, your components are seeing the same current as they would see at full throttle during the instant there is a power on pulse. For that reason, you should make sure all the components in your power system are rated for the current pulled at full throttle. Using undersized components because you never fly at full throttle is a mistake when using these digital devices.

## Programming ESC Variables

Nearly all ESCs have programming variables you can select to customize the ESC's operation for your particular need. This helps better match the wide array of motors and manufacturers a particular ESC might be paired with. Programming can be done using the transmitter, using a programming card or in some cases by connecting the ESC to a computer via a special cable. Even when the defaults listed for the ESC suit your purposes, use the basic throttle calibration process for your ESC to ensure the ESC senses the actual limits of your transmitter's throttle channel. When using the transmitter to calibrate and program your model, be sure to remove the propeller.

## Throttle Calibration

When setting up your model with a new transmitter, most ESC manufacturers recommend calibrating the throttle range. In most cases, this includes turning on the transmitter and moving the throttle stick to full open or 100%. Next, power on the model using the battery. The ESC will beep a couple of times and then you'll move the throttle to fully closed or 0%. The ESC will again beep signaling the throttle range has been captured. Use the directions that came with your ESC to validate its specific procedures.

Calibrating the throttle will ensure that the ESC provides full power at the full power throttle setting. Failure to do this could result in the ESC providing less than full power when the throttle is positioned at full open.

## Transmitter Programming

Programmable ESCs can be programmed using the transmitter and throttle stick. This is a tedious process that demands your full attention. It's not hard, it's just, well, a pain. Again, remove the propeller before programming. When using the transmitter programming method, you'll place the throttle at full open with the transmitter on before plugging in the model. When powered on, the ESC will beep as when calibrating the throttle. Wait a few more seconds. The ESC will then play a short series of tones in a little tune.

After the tune plays the ESC will cycle through a series of beeps. A single beep is for programming option one, two beeps for option two and so on. When you reach the option you wish to program, you'll move the stick to full down. At that point the ESC will again loop through a series of tones representing the choices for that option. When you hear the tone count that corresponds to the setting you want, move the throttle back to full open. After a moment the programming tune will play and the ESC will again begin cycling through the choices. If you miss the count just wait for the series to begin again.

With up to eight top-level variables to choose from, you can see that this is a tedious process.

## Card Programming

Some ESC manufacturers also make small cards that make programming your ESC much easier. Some programming cards use battery power from a receiver pack and have a number of LEDs that light up next to the various programmable functions. You can use input buttons on the card to cycle through the choices and select the options you need. When you've made your selections you'll press an OK or similarly labeled button and the settings will be transferred to the ESC.

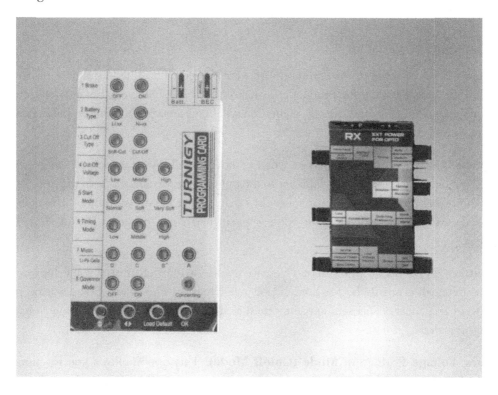

Figure 13.3. LED and jumper style ESC programming cards.

Other programming cards use jumper-style switches to select the programming options you have. Once you've placed the jumpers between the pins corresponding to your choices, plug the ESC line to the receiver into the programming card and plug in the model's main battery. The ESC will beep and you're done. Just power things down, remove the ESC line from the card and reconnect it to the receiver. The down side to using these programming cards is that they often don't work with other brands or even other series of ESCs from the same manufacture. The good news is that they're cheap.

## PC Programming

Some more expensive ESCs are also programmable via your personal computer. With these ESCs you're able to program the usual settings along with more advanced settings found on more expensive ESCs. In some cases, you're also able to update the ESC's firmware. When using this method, you must connect the ESC to your computer via a special cable or USB converter provided by the ESC's manufacturer. You'll also use the software provided by that manufacture. In most cases, you'll get that software by visiting the downloads or support page of their website and installing it on your computer.

With all these programming methods, be sure to follow the instructions provided with your particular device. They will be similar but perhaps not exactly as described here depending on what manufacturer produced your ESC.

## Common ESC Variables

Here is a list of some of the common ESC variables you'll be able to program on your ESC. Be sure to look at the product information that came with your ESC to determine whether anything beyond throttle calibration will be necessary. Oftentimes, the defaults will be right for your needs.

**Brake**. This option allows you to set whether the ESC will allow the motor to spin in the airflow or if it will apply enough power to the right motor windings to hold the prop still. Windmilling propellers will cause more drag than a static prop. Activating the brake on an electric sailplane will allow the wind to push the folding propeller back against the nose.

**Battery Type**. This option allows you to set the battery chemistry you'll be using. Defaults will normally be for lithium polymer batteries. The other choice will be for NiCad and NiMH. This setting is important as it will determine the proper low voltage cutoff setting.

**Low Voltage Protection Mode (Cutoff Mode)**. This option allows you to choose whether the motor just stops when the low voltage cutoff (LVC) target is reached or whether it will start producing noticeably less power as the battery approaches the low voltage cutoff. My preference is the gradual reduction. It will normally give you time to maneuver for an approach and landing.

**Low Voltage Protection Threshold**. This option allows you to select the low voltage cutoff target. With lipo batteries, you'll want an LVC of 3.1 volts or more per cell. Lipos can be damaged when cell voltage drops below 3.0 volts. You may want to choose the high limit to give yourself some extra leeway. This option reads the battery chemistry from the battery type selection since NiCad and NiMH LVCs are different.

**Startup Mode**. This option determines how long the motor will take to spin up. Soft and Super Soft settings are used for helicopters with heavier rotor systems.

**Timing**. The timing option is determined by the number of poles in the brushless motor you are using. Think magnet poles. The low setting is best for motors with 2 poles. With more than 2 poles, the medium setting will normally produce the best performance. With lots of poles and when you desire high speeds, you may wish to try the high setting.

## Using your ESC

Once you have your ESC properly programmed and have completed the throttle calibration, you're ready to go. The settings won't change between uses so you'll be ready to go quickly each time you fly.

Safety dictates that you first turn on you transmitter and have it set to the correct model. Then, while staying out of the way of the propeller, plug in the main battery. Your ESC should emit a tone and it will beep for each of the battery cells it detects. If you are using a three cell lipo, you'll hear three beeps then a longer tone indicating the ESC is ready.

Different manufacturers use different alert signals. Check the paper work on your specific ESC. Some of the alert tones you'll notice are a low voltage alert, a no throttle signal alert and a throttle not closed alert. Any of these conditions will keep your ESC from arming.

For example, you may get the low voltage alert if you grabbed a discharged battery. The no throttle alert occurs if you have forgotten to turn on the transmitter first or if the ESC lead to the receiver is not connected. You can also get this alert when the transmitter and receiver are too close together and they don't bind. Obviously, the throttle not closed alert occurs when the throttle is someplace other than closed or off. Always touch the throttle stick to make sure it is all the way down. Even one click of throttle will cause the alert to sound.

Some manufacturers have an emergency reserve function programmed into their ESCs. If you fly your model until the low voltage cutoff is activated, you can get another 30 seconds to a minute of motor power by bringing the throttle to idle and then back up. This is especially handy if you have your ESC programmed to abruptly cut motor power when reaching the LVC. With this function you can maneuver without power toward the runway with the throttle in idle then add power as necessary for landing. More than a few models have landed short of the runway or crashed because the pilot didn't know about this emergency reserve.

## Linear Battery Eliminator Circuits

Battery Eliminator Circuits come in one of two forms: linear or switching. Regardless of form, the BEC allows the modeler to avoid using a receiver battery and adding the weight the extra battery entails. Let's take a look at linear BECs first.

Many small capacity BECs use linear voltage regulators to drop the voltage down to the approximately 5 volts that RC receivers need. They do this by using a resistor to convert the excess voltage into heat and pass along the 5 volts to the receiver.

When you use a battery with more cells (volts) the BEC has more heat to dissipate. Heat is not a friend to electronic circuits. Placing a load via the receiver (the servos) plus the heat from the resistor has the potential to trip the temperature sensor on the ESC causing it to shut down. Your BEC may also shut down due to overheating. It should come back on almost immediately but signal loss to some 2.4 GHz receivers could mean several seconds of no control while the receiver reconnects to the transmitter.

You will also see manufacturers include servo limits in the materials that accompany an ESC with a BEC. You'll see lower servo counts go along with higher cell counts. The higher the voltage, the lower the number of servos the model should have. All that in an effort to reduce heat.

Small ESCs usually have BECs capable of producing 5 volts and handling 2-3 amps. The ESC product information on its product page online or included with its packaging will list capacities and limitations. Larger ESCs many have linear BECs capable of handling 4 amps. By the time you're looking at ESCs in the 40 – 60 amp range, you'll also notice that the BECs change to switching technologies.

## Switching Battery Eliminator Circuits

Switching BECs use the same electrical technique used in the ESC portion of the combined devices to provide voltage to the receiver. Rather than use an analog resistor to drop the voltage and dissipate excess voltage as heat, the switching BEC switches the current flow on and off very fast. A control circuit ensures the output voltage is seen as 5 volts at the receiver. These circuits are much more efficient but also more expensive. That's why you start to see them on higher capacity and higher priced ESCs.

Larger models often have more servos and other devices such as electric landing gear retract systems besides having larger motors. All these require power. Switching BECs will not normally have the servo restrictions that linear BECs will have since heat is not as big an issue.

## External BECs

Many modelers prefer to use external BECs rather than the ones included on the ESC. These BECs are sometimes referred to as Universal BECs (UBECs) or Switching BECs (SBECs). Larger ESCs can also have switching BECs as we just discussed but some manufacturers may want to emphasize the switching technology used on their external BECs.

External BECs can be found as either linear or switching. Small capacity, inexpensive external BECs are usually linear and can output 3 amps at 5 volts. External BECs that can accept high voltage inputs and have switch selectable outputs of 5 or 6 volts are usually switching BECs. These external BECs will often be able to output 5 amps.

For extremely power hungry models, you can find external BECs that will accept 50 volts input and output up to 9 volts at 20 amps.

Many modelers believe using external BECs is safer. They fear that a failure in the ESC could also cause a failure in the onboard BEC. There is certainly some truth to that. In one instance, I saw an ESC failure that produced so much heat the battery input wire solder joints melted and the battery wires disconnected from the ESC circuit board. Obviously, that ended with a crash.

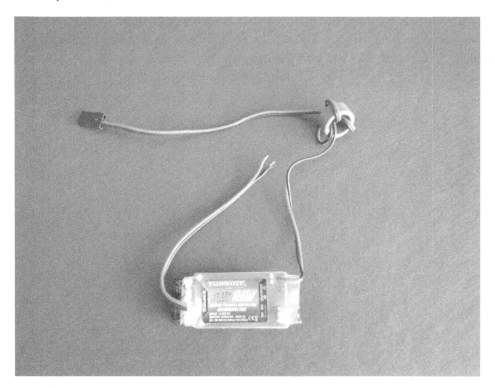

Figure 13.4. An external Universal BEC or UBEC.

External BECs separate the two components so an ESC failure will not result in the loss of receiver power and thus the loss of control. External BECs are wired directly into the main power circuit between the battery and ESC. This is done either by directly soldering the external BEC's inputs to the battery connector on the ESC or by inserting a small pass through connector with a tap that can be connected to the external BEC. You can use these same techniques when using an external BEC with an ESC that doesn't have an onboard BEC.

## Closing

The ESC and BECs are a couple of the more complex components of your model. Knowing their capabilities and limitations are critical for enjoying your model to the fullest. As with many electronic devices, operating well within the manufacturer's capacity limits is a good technique to ensure optimum performance and long component life.

A ten to twenty percent capacity surplus is a good idea and is not very expensive. If you anticipate your model will pull 30 amps or you plan to target that level, a 40 amp ESC would be a good choice. Same with the BEC. If you have six or seven servos and electric retracts with some onboard telemetry, spend a few extra dollars and use an external BEC with at least five amps of output. You'll wish you had when you notice the 'magic smoke' trailing your aircraft and you no longer have aircraft control. Trust me. I speak from experience.

# 14 Battery Basics

Batteries are to electric models as glow fuel and gasoline are to internal combustion engine powered RC models. There are a variety of battery chemistries that you will come across. Each tends to have specific uses in todays' electric models. Let's take a look at the common battery types used in RC models and some pros and cons to each.

## Nickel Cadmium and Nickel Metal Hydride

NiCad and NiMH batteries are some of the early rechargeable battery chemistries. Being rechargeable made them valuable for early electric modelers and they remain valuable as receiver battery packs today. NiCad and NiMH batteries produce 1.2 volts per cell. You're probably familiar with these batteries and the common AA and AAA sizes found in electronics or hardware stores. They can replace disposable alkaline batteries as they have a similar voltage and size factor.

International standards for this battery type include many more sizes than just AA and AAA. Early models used a variety of sizes bundled into packs that fit the space in the model. Some modelers purchased individual cells and soldered them together to meet their specific needs.

Whether purchased as packs or built at home, these packs share a common feature. They are assembled in series to increase the voltage to the desired level. Due to their weight and size, battery packs using this chemistry normally didn't go beyond 8 cells or 9.6 volts. With small electric motors rated at 6 to 7.2 volts this was not an issue. Brushless motors capable of accepting upwards of 50 volts changed that.

The advantage to both these chemistries is that they are easily and safely rechargeable. Their chargers are simple devices and the batteries can be left on them overnight to be ready to go in the morning. The down side is that their capacity is limited and packs with high voltage outputs are not practical. NiCad batteries had the additional problem of developing a memory effect. When discharged to the same extent over several cycles, the battery 'remembers' when it will be recharged and suffers a voltage drop at that point even when the rated capacity is higher. Modelers deal with this by fully discharging packs before recharging. Many battery chargers have built in cycling routines that will discharge and then recharge NiCad packs to prevent memory effect. NiMH batteries do not suffer from this problem.

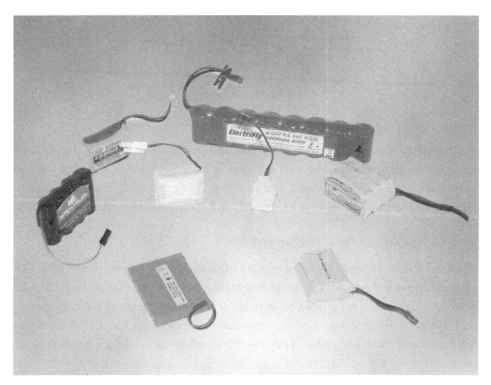

Figure 14.1. A variety of NiMH and NiCad packs with various cell sizes.

## Lithium Iron Phosphate

LiFe batteries are a bit newer on the RC scene. These batteries are proving to be very popular with modelers who want an improved experience with receiver and transmitter batteries.

LiFe batteries appear much like lithium polymer batteries. That is, they are constructed from flat cells wired together in series and wrapped in a lightweight plastic shrink wrap material. LiFe batteries produce 3.3 volts per cell and are usually found in two or three cell packs.

A big advantage of LiFe batteries over NiMH is power density. The amount of energy per unit of weight is much higher. Other advantages include lighter weight, faster charge time, even discharge voltage and they can hold their charge longer between uses.

Multi-chemistry chargers usually have a setting for LiFe batteries. Otherwise, LiFe specific chargers are available.

## Lithium Polymer

Together with low-cost brushless DC motors, lipo batteries have driven the burgeoning popularity of electric RC airplanes. Lipos can be found in a wide variety of capacities and voltages. Together with their high power density, lipos make electric powered RC airplanes a strong competitor with models powered by internal combustion engines.

For most of us, the terms Lithium Polymer and Lithium Ion mean the same thing. At a practical level they are the same. Technically, however, they do differ in the way they are assembled and in terms of the electrolyte used. Additionally, lithium ion batteries are placed in hard cases while lithium polymer cells are often found in foil packets or pouches. For our purpose, we'll use the term lithium polymer (lipo) and will be referring to the pouch-type cells used in RC flying.

Each lipo cell has a nominal voltage of 3.7 volts per cell. That means multi-cell battery packs are described in increments of 3.7 volts. For example, a two-cell pack is described as producing 7.4 volts and a four-cell pack is described as having 14.8 volts. In practice, a fully charged cell will read between 4.1 and 4.2 volts so that four-cell pack will show as high as 16.8 volts or so when fully charged.

Lithium polymer packs have several important operating limitations. These include discharge limits, charge and discharge rate limits and proper storage voltage.

## Discharge Limits

Lipos cannot be fully discharged without damaging or destroying the battery. Lipos should not be discharged below 3 volts per cell. Discharging your battery to this level will cause heat buildup and may cause the battery cells to puff up. That is why setting the low-voltage cutoff on your plane's ESC is so important. Many modelers plan their flights to use no more than approximately 80% of the battery's capacity. This leaves time for a missed approach while still landing well within the battery's discharge limit. Flying until the low voltage cutoff occurs is hard on lipo batteries and will limit their useful life.

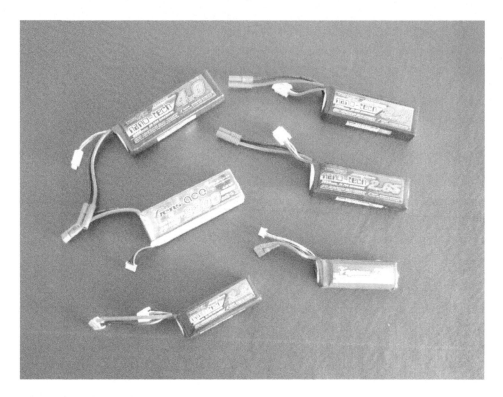

Figure 14.2. A variety of small to medium sized lithium polymer batteries.

## Charge Rate Limits

Lipo batteries also have limits on how fast they can be charged and discharged. On the charging side, early batteries could only be charged at 1C. 'C' is a term that refers to the battery's current flow capacity. In this case, a 2200 milliamp hour (mAh) battery should be charged at a rate no higher than 2.2 amps. Improvements in battery technology now allow batteries to be charged at multiples of their C rating. Be sure to check your battery manufacturer's recommendations. A recent survey of several battery brands showed many still recommended 1C charging. Several allowed for 2C to 5C charging. Higher charge rates will cut the charge time but many modelers believe it also shortens battery life. Many still make it a practice to charge at the 1C rate even with batteries that allow higher charge rates.

Additionally, lipo batteries have to be charged using chargers especially designed for lipo batteries. The charger needs to be able to assess the battery's charge state and shut off once it reaches its capacity. Overcharged lipo batteries can heat up and rupture their cases or pouches. When the inner material is exposed to air, it flares up and can catch fire in addition to venting lots of smoke. For this reasons you should charge your batteries on fireproof surfaces and use safety techniques such as using fireproof lipo battery bags. You should also not leave your batteries unattended while charging. That is not to say you have to stare at them for an hour, but be close by so you can react to any charger alert tones or battery venting events. As always, follow both battery manufacturer's and charger manufacturer's instructions.

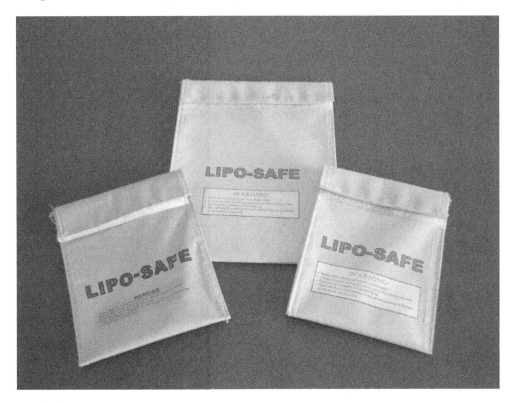

Figure 14.3. Fire resistant charging bags come in a variety of sizes.

Lipo batteries should be balanced as they charge. The best solution is to use a charger with a built in balancing circuit. These are very common, even in low priced chargers. This allows the charger to monitor each cell's capacity to ensure no cell is overcharged. With these chargers, the battery's discharge plug is connected to the main charge connector and the battery's balance tap is connected to the socket for the number of cells the battery has. This can also be done with a small balancing device plugged into the battery's balance tap. These devices can be used with or without a charger. They use circuits to direct energy from the battery's more highly charged cells to its less charged cells. Thus the term 'balancing.' For example, you can use one to balance a pack after flight if you see one cell has several tenths of a volt difference than the others in the pack. Your first choice when charging should be to use a charger with an integrated balancing circuit. See Chapter 18 for more on chargers and balancing gadgets.

Serious injuries, deaths and significant property damage have occurred when lipo batteries were not charged correctly. Pay attention to what you are doing.

## Discharge Rate Limits

Discharge rate limitations also apply. You will notice that batteries are not only sold by their capacity but also by their C rating. Batteries with higher C ratings allow faster discharging but cost more. The standard formula to compute a battery's discharge rate in amps is to multiply the capacity in milliamp hours by the C rating and divide by 1000. Let's assume we have a 2200 mAh battery with a 25 C rating. 2200 times 25 equals 55,000. Divide 55,000 by 1000 and you'll get 55. Fifty-five represents the maximum continuous amps the battery should be called upon to produce. I've found this is a bit generous. I'll normally plan to use only about 80% of that value. You can compute the maximum burst amperage the same way. Just use the burst rate C rating in the computation.

In the typical RC application, batteries will try to deliver all the power you are asking for. If you are asking for too much, the battery limits can be exceeded and damage occur. Be sure you are aware of the current flows your power setup is demanding before flying. While a smoking, flaming streak of debris across the sky is very dramatic, knowing it is your model can put a damper on the flying day. We'll discuss this in more detail in Chapter 17.

## Storage Limits

Lipos aren't meant to be charged and set on the shelf for future use. Most modelers will charge their batteries no earlier than the night before they plan to use them. Batteries stored for long periods can lose their effectiveness. Storage voltage for lipo cells is 3.85 volts per cell. Some chargers can be set to charge your battery to the storage level. For example if cold weather limits your flying season you can set your charger to the storage setting at the end of the flying season, charge to that level, then put your batteries away till spring. If you will be flying again in a couple of days, just leave the battery at the same voltage it had when you landed and put it on the charger just before you fly.

## Safety Practices

Besides the operational limits we've discussed already, there are several other safety-related issues regarding lipo use. Here are a few:

Don't charge your lipo in your car or in your model. As we've discussed, charging accidents do happen and the heat and flame from a venting lipo can destroy your vehicle or model.

Do charge your batteries using a lipo charger at a safe location. A concrete driveway or pad away from the house or vehicle is a good choice. Using lipo bags or concrete blocks set to make small vaults for the batteries are both good practices.

Do discard lipo batteries only when fully discharged. You can do that by using a small load on the battery. An example might be an automotive light bulb wired directly to the battery leads. Some manufacturers recommend placing the battery in salt water when at very low voltages to completely drain the cells. Regardless, the batteries are safe to discard in the trash when fully drained. Another good option is to make use of battery disposal and recycling services at some retailers. They'll know how to handle the battery safely and you'll be rid of it quickly. Again, follow manufacturer's recommendations.

Do discard damaged lipos. Crashes can and do happen. Damaged lipos should not be used. Damage can include bent or crushed cells, excessive puffing and so on. If you damage your lipo, place it in a safe place (like a bucket of sand) for about a half an hour. If it hasn't vented, transport it in a fire proof container to where you can prepare it for disposal. Don't be the person who sets the club shade structure or trash dumpster on fire by simply throwing your battery in the trash with no preparation.

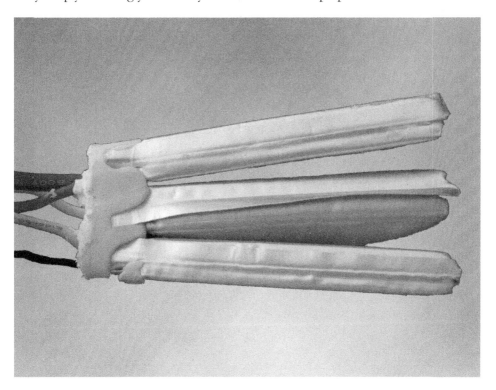

Figure 14.4. A puffed lipo cell. Note how the center cell has expanded.

Don't puncture puffed packs. When lipos are abused they sometimes puff up. While minor puffing won't prevent further use, extreme puffing should result in your discharging and disposing of the battery. It may be tempting to puncture the foil to release the pressure. Don't. Remember the chemicals used in the lipo burn when exposed to air. Even a little pin prick can set them off.

## Closing

Lithium polymer batteries got a bit of a bad reputation when they first appeared and modelers failed to deal with them properly. Using NiCad chargers, charging in cars and not paying attention to pack balance states were common violations. Unfortunately, those violations sometimes carried a heavy price including fire-damaged homes and vehicles, and even deaths. With ongoing education and greater familiarity with these little powerhouses, incident rates have declined and folks are more likely to speak up if they see someone about to do something foolish.

Vendors sell millions of these batteries and modelers fly hundreds of flights per battery. They are not the danger some might want you to believe while at the same time they are not the casual tool that others suggest. Know their limitations and treat them with respect as you would any powerful tool.

# 15 Propeller Basics

With electric powered models, without propellers nothing flies. Even with electric ducted fan powered jet models, the fan is a propeller. Propellers are a science. They include aerodynamics, advanced mathematics and even a bit of weather. Oh, and did I mention a smidgeon of Mach? You can choose to go as deeply into the subject as your interest and engineering skills allow. We, however, going to stay up near the surface of this deep body of knowledge.

## Diameter

As we discussed in an earlier chapter, propellers used in RC modeling are described using two numbers such as 9 X 6. The first number is the propeller's diameter and the second is the propeller's pitch. In this example the unit of measure is inches. You will find propellers using metric measures too.

Diameter is a pretty easy concept. It is simply the length of a straight line passing through the center of a circle. Since a two-bladed prop is a straight line, you can simply measure the distance from tip to tip. On a three-bladed prop, the blades aren't opposite each other so you'll need to measure the radius (center to a blade tip) and double it. The prop's diameter impacts performance. The larger the diameter the more air it will move given a constant pitch when compared to a smaller diameter prop. Additionally, the larger the diameter the faster the tip speed for a given motor RPM. Again, assuming a constant pitch, a larger diameter prop will produce more resistance requiring more amps for a given RPM.

## Pitch

Pitch refers to the size of the bite the propeller takes as it rotates. The simple way to think about pitch is that it is the distance a propeller would pull forward through a soft solid like gelatin in one revolution. A propeller with a pitch of six would advance six inches per revolution. With our models, low pitch props are better for applications including stunts and aerobatics. Low pitch props can accelerate faster and allow for the quick changes in direction often required in aerobatics. High pitch props are best for speed applications. High pitch props will pull more amps vs. a lower pitched prop of the same diameter. With that in mind, motor heat can become a problem if you are really trying to squeeze every ounce of speed from your set-up.

For sport flyers and new pilots, consider a propeller pitch about 70% of the diameter. For example, you'd get good performance from a propeller with a 10-inch diameter and a 7-inch pitch. It is not unusual to see trainer ARF packages with pitch to diameter ratios of .5 to .7.

## Blades

Most of the time, using a two-bladed propeller will be your first choice. Assuming you have chosen one recommended in the motor product information, you can expect your best overall efficiency. There are some good reasons to consider three-bladed propellers too. Generally speaking, the three-bladed propeller will not be as efficient as a two-bladed one. If you are a beginner that won't matter. You will probably be flying fairly conservatively anyway. A big reason to use a three-bladed prop is clearance. Just like with full scale airplanes such as World War II fighters, there is only so much room between the motor shaft at the center of the propeller and the ground. This is especially true when the tail is up as in takeoff or landing. This is also true with twin-engine airplanes such as a DC-3. Not only are there ground clearance issues, there's also fuselage clearance issues.

There are also vanity issues. Lots of modelers want their models to look like their full scale counterparts. If the full scale aircraft flies with a three-bladed prop, they want their model to as well.

As a rule of thumb, when converting from a two bladed prop to a three bladed one, consider increasing the propeller's pitch an inch for every inch you decrease the diameter. For example, if your motor manufacturer recommends an 11 X 7 inch two-bladed prop with a particular voltage applied to the motor, you would choose a 10 X 8 three-bladed prop to get about the same performance.

While normally not an issue with small to medium sized electric models, going to a three-bladed prop will also reduce tip speed. Since the diameter of the propeller's disk is smaller the tip speed will be lower given a constant motor RPM. Propellers become much less efficient as they reach the transonic speed range. As speed increases into this transonic range, they also create shock waves that can make the model too noisy for some flying locations. This can be an issue for large diameter props on models powered by internal combustion engines.

## RPM limits

Propellers have RPM limits. You can find the limits by visiting the web page of your propeller manufacturer. RPM limits are normally described as a fairly large number divided by propeller diameter. You can think of that large number as being the RPM limit of a 1 inch propeller. For example, propeller manufacturer APC suggests propeller limits for their thin electric propellers as 145,000 / prop diameter. That means a 10 inch propeller would have a limiting RPM of 14,500. That also means that if you have a 1000 Kv motor you'd exceed the propeller's safety limit with 14.8 volts applied to the motor. If you were planning on using a 4 cell lipo, you'd want to consider using a smaller prop or lower Kv motor. Remember tip speed goes down with a smaller diameter as the limiting RPM goes up.

Here are some representative numbers pulled from various manufacturers' product information. As always, refer to your specific manufacturer's product data.

Slow flyer props – 65,000 / prop diameter

Thin electric – 145,000 / prop diameter

Multi rotor – 105,000 / prop diameter

Glass-filled nylon – 165,000 / prop diameter

## Propeller Types

Besides the number of blades, there are several other options for the electric modeler to choose from when selecting a propeller. Here are a couple of them.

## Slow Flyer

Slow flyer props are designed especially for slow flying electric models. They can be easily identified by their wide blades. Slow flyer props assume lower RPM motors. While they have the same naming convention in terms of diameter and pitch, they are lighter weight and have much lower RPM limits.

## Thin Electric

Thin electric props are the mainstay of electric model propellers. They are found in a multitude of diameters and pitch combinations. Their higher RPM limits allow their use with a wide range of voltages and motor Kv ratings. As the name suggests, they have fairly thin blades when compared to slow flyer props. While the blades are thinner, they are stiffer allowing for higher RPM limits.

## Folding

Folding propellers have screws or pins connecting the propeller blade to the propeller's hub. This creates a hinge allowing the propeller to fold back against the plane's fuselage. Folding props are used primarily with sailplanes. When the motor is spinning, centrifugal force causes the blades to extend and provide thrust for the model. Electric powered sailplanes will normally have the ESC brake set to 'on' causing the prop to stop spinning when the motor does. The wind will then blow the blades back against the fuselage. This reduces drag allowing the glider to be more efficient.

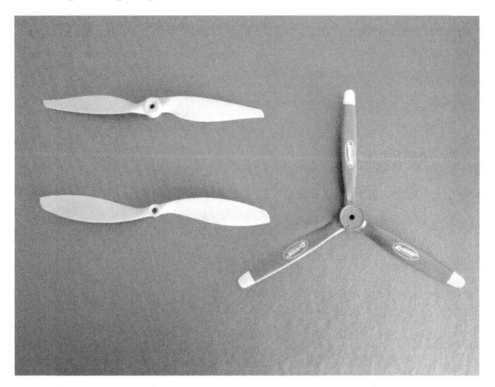

Figure 15.1. Various propellers. Note the large flat blades of the slow flyer prop.

## Counter Rotating

Counter rotating props are built with the pitch reversed from normal propellers. They are normally used in twin engine applications to cancel the rolling effect of torque most noticeable during takeoff. A counter rotating prop will be set to spin opposite its normal spinning partner.

## Impellers

Impellers are the rapidly spinning inner core of electric ducted fan power systems. They are matched to the diameter of the EDF unit itself. Impellers for ducted fan units come with anywhere from three to a dozen blades. Due to their small size they usually are found coupled to motors with moderate to high Kv ratings. They spin very fast. RPM limits on ducted fan units seem settle at about 45,000. You'll need to multiply your anticipated voltage by the motor Kv to ensure you remain within limits. As with other propellers, larger units will pull more amps. You'll need to manage current and your battery's voltage and C rating in addition to RPM.

## Propeller Balancing

Many propellers you buy will need a little work to bring them into balance. Balance is important in that out of balance propellers will cause vibrations that can cause things to come loose. Prop nuts, motor mount screws and a variety of other things can all loosen to disastrous effect. In some extreme cases, an out of balance prop can literally tear the nose off the model.

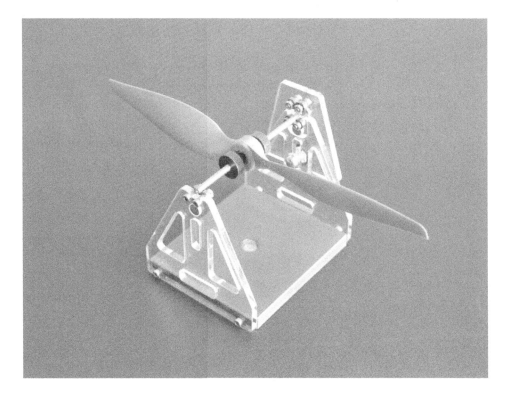

Figure 15.2. Thin electric prop on a balancing stand. This prop is balanced.

Fortunately, balancing props is pretty simple. Several suppliers have prop balancing stands. These stands usually include a small stand with either magnets or bearings mounted on the sides with an axle placed between them. The axle is placed through the hub of the propeller being balanced and placed between the stand's two supports. The prop's heavy side will fall. Using magnets or low friction bearings to suspend the axle allows you to notice even slight differences. You can get a fingertip balancer for your field box to use in a pinch (no pun intended). You simply mount the propeller on the axle and pinch it between your fingers and see what end drops. This tool will have more friction to overcome so won't be as accurate as using a stand. Go with a stand if you can.

Once you have identified the propeller's heavy side, there are several techniques to bring it into balance. You can either add weight to the light side or remove weight from the heavy side. For your electric slow flyer simply add a piece of tape to the back of the lighter blade and recheck the balance. Add larger pieces until it balances. On larger or faster planes, you can add a thin coat of varnish or CA adhesive to the back side. The varnish or CA shouldn't change the shape of the blade, just add a little weight. Again, recheck and adjust as necessary. You could also paint the tips of the props. This is a good safety precaution anyway. Just add a couple of more coats to the light side to bring the prop into balance.

## Closing

There is a lot to consider when choosing a propeller for your model. Fortunately, motor manufacturers help make it easy with recommended prop sizes based on voltage or cell counts. Your propeller is the primary source of resistance in your electrical system. Changing the prop will result in changes to other electrical properties. You should measure those differences to ensure the power system will still operate within limits.

# 16 Receiver Basics

Your model's receiver translates the signal from your transmitter into inputs to the various electronic devices in your model. These devices include things like the throttle control, various servos and landing gear retract systems. Not only does the receiver pass along the control signals, for most RC airplanes, it also provides power to the components. Power supplied to the receiver by either the ESC's BEC or an external BEC is passed along to all the components connected to the receiver. Let's take a quick look at the receivers you're likely to run across.

## 72 MHz Receivers

If you are using a 72 MHz transmitter you'll need a receiver matched to that band. Older basic 72 MHz transmitters often transmit an AM signal. If you have one of those transmitters, you'll need an AM receiver. Other 72 MHz transmitters use FM signals. In those cases, you'll need FM receivers. Since 72 MHz transmitters are configured to broadcast on an authorized RC frequency, the transmitter and receiver must be set to the same channel.

Most 72 MHz receivers use a crystal to control their frequency response. Crystals are usually sold separately and mount on the receiver. There may be size issues from manufacturer to manufacturer so a crystal from one brand may not fit in another. Some 72 MHz receivers use an electronic circuit to control the frequency it responds to. These synthetic receivers can be programmed to respond to any of the authorized channels using your transmitter and a programming procedure specific to that receiver.

Many computer-type 72 MHz FM transmitters can be set to transmit a Pulse Position Modulation signal or a Pulse Code Modulation signal. PPM is normally just referred to as FM. PCM signals contain a digital signal within the FM signal that allows for less impact from signal noise and interference. You'll see plain FM and PCM receivers.

You'll need a PCM receiver for the transmitter to work in the PCM mode. If you are planning on using a 72MHz transmitter, review its manual to clarify its PCM settings and requirements. For a beginner using a hand-me-down transmitter, PPM or plain FM is sufficient.

Normally, 72 MHz receivers do not require a specific brand of transmitter. For example, you could use a Hitec FM receiver with an FM transmitter from another manufacturer. With the popularity of 2.4 GHz radio systems, new 72 MHz receivers are getting hard to find. You can, however, find some good deals at swap meets.

## Ham Band Receivers

Licensed amateur radio operators may use portions of the 50 MHz band to operate model aircraft. The radio system must include a transmitter capable of transmitting in the 50 MHz band. For all practical purposes, radio systems in this frequency band work the same as FM radios in the 72 MHz band. As with the 72 MHz band, there are limited choices when shopping for 50 MHz receivers. Again, the popularity of 2.4 GHz systems is mostly to blame.

## 2.4 GHz Receivers

The most popular radio systems used in RC flying today are 2.4 GHz systems. These systems operate in authorized space in the 2.4 GHz frequency band. 2.4 GHz receivers provide the same function as their 72 MHz cousins. They receive the control signals from the transmitter and pass them along to the appropriate component. They also distribute electrical power to the electronic components.

Where they differ is how they connect with the transmitter. This starts to get complicated so we'll stay at a pretty high level.

Unlike radio systems in the 72 MHz band, 2.4 GHz systems don't transmit on a single frequency within the band. For this reason, there are no numbered channels associated with 2.4 GHz systems and no need for frequency control boards at the RC field. You don't have to worry about radio interference from another transmitter causing your airplane to crash. This is a huge part of these systems' popularity. Current 2.4 GHz systems use a combination of spread spectrum schemes to achieve this.

The two primary techniques of making use of the entire spectrum are Frequency Hopping Spread Spectrum and Direct Sequence Spread Spectrum. Frequency Hopping Spread Spectrum uses a technique where the transmitter and the receiver hop in unison from one frequency to another very quickly. Data is passed before each hop. Hopping reduces the opportunity for interference.

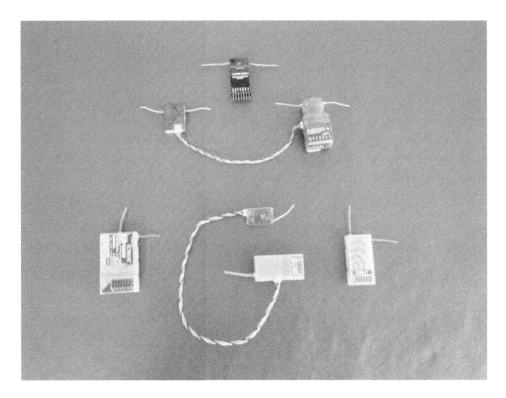

Figure 16.1. A variety of Spektrum and Spektrum compatible receivers.

In Direct Sequence Spread Spectrum, the transmitter and receiver start at a common channel within the band and are aware of a code describing the channel order used to send data. The transmitter moves according to the sequence and the receiver follows along. In this manner, even if another radio or other device is on the same frequency it would be very unlikely it would have the same data sequence code. This ability to focus on data at specific points in time on a specific channel within the band proved to have an additional advantage – greater range. Receivers could decode messages further out than frequency hopping systems alone due to their ability to limit the impact of noise in the signal.

After gaining some experience with their first generation of 2.4 GHz spread spectrum RC radio systems, major manufacturers made changes. They ended up taking the best from both techniques and combining them. Nowadays, most 2.4 GHz radio systems use both frequency hopping and direct sequence techniques. For example, Futaba added direct sequence techniques with its upgraded FASST systems and Spektrum and JR added frequency hopping with their DSM2, DSMX and DSSS systems. Other major manufacturers do the same thing in one form or another.

Entire books have been written about the technical intricacies of spread spectrum technologies. Having condensed this down to a couple of sentences in non-technical language will obviously leave some gaps. There are lots of resources available to you to feed your inner geek on the specifics of these spread spectrum technologies. Check out your favorite bookseller or online search engine to dig deeper.

Since different manufacturers implement their spread spectrum radio systems differently, receivers from one manufacturer will not work with a competing manufacturer's systems. There are some exceptions so be sure to double check. Additionally there are third party manufacturers who sell receivers designed to interact with specific brand name radio systems while not carrying that same brand name. These receivers are often much less expensive than their name brand counterparts.

Third party receivers and counterfeit receivers are not the same. As with all online shopping, name brand receivers at rock bottom prices should be viewed with caution.

The availability of these third party receivers may influence your choice of radio system. This is much like using a third party or non-OEM fender when repairing accident damage to your car. You may feel strongly about using OEM parts so you might feel strongly about using brand specific receivers. If that is the case, you can be sure that any of the major manufacturers' radio systems will serve you well.

On the other hand, if you think your journey in the hobby may include a bunch of small foamies filling your hangar to overflowing, you may find that putting an $80 receiver into a $25 foam profile model doesn't make much sense. For you, settling on a brand with good, inexpensive third party options may be a better choice.

From a performance standpoint, there just isn't much difference with the major manufacturers' products. Each will provide a solid link between the transmitter and the receiver. Availability, looks, weight, feel and quality construction are more important considerations than any specific spread spectrum technique.

## Special Considerations

Many 2.4 GHz receivers will either come with a pair of antennas pointing different directions or with a satellite receiver attachment. Having a second antenna oriented in a different geometric plane increases signal reception. Satellite receivers should be placed with their antennas pointing 90 degrees from the antenna on the primary receiver.

Foam, balsa and fiberglass materials are porous enough for radio signals to penetrate easily. Models constructed with carbon fiber or with carbon fiber components near the receiver can block signals in the 2.4 GHz band. Most major manufacturers have receivers especially designed for these applications. When shopping for these receivers, look for the ones with longer antenna leads. That will be an easy tip off.

All 2.4 GHz receivers need to be bound to their respective transmitters. Binding procedures vary from brand to brand but the purpose is the same. By binding the receiver to the transmitter, the key codes and sequences for the spread spectrum techniques used by that radio system are paired between the transmitter and receiver. The receiver will then be able to identify and interpret the signals from that specific transmitter.

Various manufacturers produce receivers for small aircraft. You may see these listed as 'Micro,' 'Nano' or 'Park Flyer.' These receivers have limited range and should not be used on large models. They are great for indoor models and small 3D foamies but not for larger models.

## Channels

Regardless of frequency band, each action on your model will require a receiver channel. A basic trainer with ailerons, rudder, elevator and throttle will require four channels. If your model has a servo for each aileron and you want to adjust each one separately, each servo will require a separate channel. Now you're up to five. If you want flaps or retractable landing gear, they'll each need a channel too. By the time you get to nice scale models with sequenced gear doors and other scale effects, you can quickly get up to 12 to 18 channels. Fortunately, for most of us, seven to nine channels will be plenty.

You'll be able to pick receivers with a variety of channels. Normally, you'll find receivers with three, four, six, seven and eight channels. Cost goes up with the number of channels. You'll need to have a receiver channel for each channel you plan to use on your transmitter. You do not need a nine channel receiver just because you have a nine channel transmitter. If your model only requires four channels, get a four channel receiver. The fact that the transmitter has five unused channels means nothing.

Receiver channels may be labeled with the control's name or simply numbered. For example, Spektrum labels its six channel receivers with the names for throttle, aileron, elevator, rudder, gear and aux 1. Futaba, on the other hand, simply numbers the channels. The transmitter manual will describe what number corresponds to what control or feature.

## Range Checking

You should range check your new receiver before flight and then occasionally thereafter. Different transmitter brands have slightly different procedures to range check their receivers. Most of the time the procedure involves separating the transmitter and the model with the installed receiver by a specified distance and then checking control movements while transmitting at a reduced transmitter output.

Receiver Basics

This can be done by moving the control sticks while pushing the bind button or entering the range check function on a computer radio. For 72 MHz radios, range checks are normally done with the antenna down or only one section extended. Check your transmitter manual for specifics. If the controls start to flutter or don't move at all, something is wrong. Don't fly the model until it passes the range check.

## Closing

Your model's receiver is a key element in maintaining controlled flight. Be sure you understand the limits and capacities of your device. There is not a lot you have to do with your receiver besides installing the various leads properly, positioning it thoughtfully in the model and binding it to the transmitter. Besides an occasional range check with your transmitter, there is no programming or adjusting necessary.

# 17 Putting Your Power System Together

If you have read through the previous chapters on the components that make up an electric model's power system you're probably asking yourself how this all fits together. That's the topic of this chapter. Having a good knowledge of what the components do, how they work and what some important limitations are, you're ready to connect the dots. Before we get to that, though, we need to review some key electrical terms and relationships.

## Ohm's Law

Ohm's Law is named after a German scientist who conducted measurements of applied voltage through electrical circuits in the 1820's. He described a relationship between three key components of electricity: resistance, current and voltage.

Resistance impedes the flow of electrons through the circuit. The unit of measure for resistance is named after Ohm.

Voltage is a measure of electrical potential. A voltmeter is used to measure the difference in electrical potential between two points. That difference is the voltage.

Current represents the flow of an electric charge. Like the ohm, the unit of measure for current is named after the scientist who did important work on the subject. In this case, it is named after a French scientist named Ampere.

These terms are often described using an analogy of water flowing through a garden hose. The water pressure from the faucet represents the force or the voltage in an electrical circuit. The water flowing in the hose represents the current (amps) and restrictions to the flow such as the nozzle on the end represents resistance (ohms).

Ohm's Law describes the mathematical relationship between these three forces. Amps represented by the letter I equals voltage (E) divided by resistance (R). As with any equation, you can solve for any of the values if you know two of them. So, voltage equals amps multiplied by ohms and resistance equals voltage divided by amps.

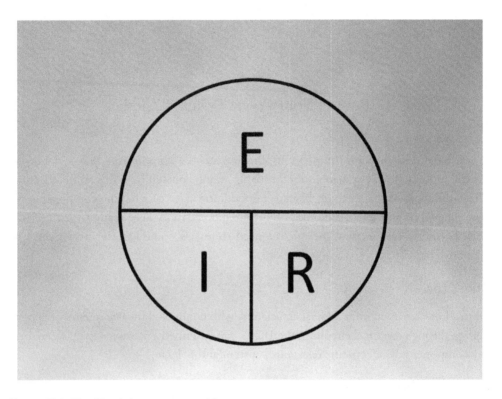

Figure 17.1. The Ohm's Law memory aid.

In the Ohm's Law illustration, the I and R are side by side representing multiplication. The E is above both the I and the R representing division. See Figure 17.1

There is one more term we need to review before moving on. That is power. Power refers to the amount of work done over a period of time. Electrical power is measured in watts. There is a similar figure to the one used to illustrate the relationship in Ohm's Law. In this case the P is placed above the I and the E. As with the Ohm's Law illustration, you can solve for any missing variable if you know the other two. The side by side placement of the I and the E represents multiplication and the P above the I and the E represents division. In this case, then, watts equals amps times voltage, amps equals watts divided by voltage and voltage equals watts divided by amps. See Figure 17.2.

As you're about to see, understanding these relationships becomes critical when choosing components for your electric model airplane or when choosing components to make upgrades to improve its performance.

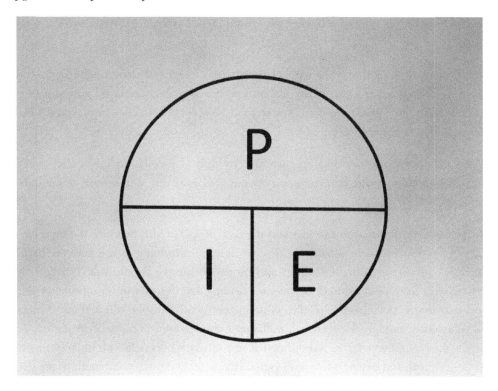

Figure 17.2. Power memory aid.

## Managing Amps

One element you'll need to manage is amps. Motors, ESCs and batteries all have amp limits that when exceeded can cause component damage or failure. We learned earlier that the formula for a battery's discharge rate limit is capacity in milliamps times C rating divided by 1000. This will give you an estimate of the amps a battery can safely deliver. Your ESC has an amp rating and the product data sheet for your motor will specify the maximum amps it can safely handle.

Your goal will be to add or subtract resistance (propeller diameter and pitch) to the circuit to achieve the desired amperage. Fortunately most motor product data sheets or online specifications will give you a place to start. They often have recommended propeller sizes based on battery voltage or cell count.

Let's say you use one of the recommended propellers. When using a 3-cell battery at 11.1 volts you pull 30 amps. You can add either prop diameter or pitch or both to increase resistance. Doing so will add to the current draw. Using a 2200 mAh battery with a 25 C rating you'd have available amps from your battery. However, if you were using a 30 amp ESC or if your motor specified a max current of 30 amps, you'd exceed those limits.

To add resistance by way of propeller size would then also require upgrades to the motor and ESC.

Well, you might think that going with a battery with a larger cell count might do the trick. Again, referring to our Ohm's Law illustration, if our resistance stayed constant (same propeller) but the voltage was increased to the 14.8 volts of a 4-cell battery, you'd still up the amps due to the increase in volts.

In our example above, our 30 amp current draw with 11.1 volts turns into a bit over 39 amps at 14.8 volts. Again, depending on the limits of your ESC and motor, you could do damage.

For practical purposes, you can just add the new propeller and measure the increase in current. To do that, place a handy RC gadget called a watt meter in line with the battery and ESC. Power up your transmitter and model and move the throttle slowly to full throttle with the model secured. If you see a reading that exceeds any components' limit, stop and return the throttle to idle. Watt meters usually display the circuit's voltage, amperage and wattage along with a milliamp-hour reading. Some will remember and display the highest levels attained during the run-up. This becomes a bit hit and miss but props are cheap and having a few with various diameter and pitch combinations are good additions to your supply box. In this way, you can zero in on the best propeller for the application you have in mind.

In the case of changing voltage, just do the math. It isn't hard. Use your voltage and amps for your current configuration to compute a resistance number. Then use that resistance to compute amperage with your new voltage.

The reverse is also true. You can reduce amperage by reducing resistance or voltage or a combination of the two. Just remember, each electrical component in your power system has an amperage limitation. All of them must be operated within the manufacturers' recommendations.

## Managing Power

You'll find several similar guidelines online and other places advising you on the watts per pound of model weight you should strive for to get a desired level of performance. For example, E-flite, a name brand manufacturer suggests the following:

50 – 70 watts per pound for very light park flyers

70 – 90 watts per pound for slow flyers and trainers

90 – 100 watts per pound for sport aerobatic planes and so on up to 200 watts per pound.

You'll need to manipulate voltage and amperage to achieve the desired wattage as those are the two elements in the power formula. First compute the total wattage necessary to give you the performance you want. Just multiply the model's weight in pounds by the desired watts per pound. While you might not be sure of the exact battery you'll be using, don't forget to add weight for your anticipated battery. You can go back and fine tune the computations after your first estimate.

With the desired total watts in mind, go shopping for a motor capable of delivering what you need. Look at the product data sheets or online specifications to help you decide. Besides wattage, consider its dimensions and other factors such as voltage limitations. Note the maximum voltage and current numbers to ensure you'll be able to achieve the wattage desired. Target an ESC for your configuration with capacity slightly above the motor's max amperage.

Now you might think that if you stay at or below the max voltage and at or below the max amperage listed for your motor you'd stay below its wattage limit. Unfortunately, that doesn't always seem to work. For example, one online vendor listed a motor's max current as 70 amps. The max voltage was listed at 19 volts. Do the math. The wattage generated at 70 amps and 19 volts equals over 1300 watts. However, the motor was listed as being able to produce only 640 watts. To get the most of the motor's available watts, you'd have to lower the voltage to 14.8 volts and prop to about 43 amps. Or, lower the voltage further to 11.1 volts and prop to about 57 amps. Depending on things like your model's ground or fuselage clearance for physical prop size, going with the higher voltage might be the best choice.

Last, double check the voltage you'll be using in terms of cell count and overall battery capacity in milliamps. Use the battery discharge formula to make sure your configuration won't overstress the battery in terms of its C rating. You'll also want to do a quick flying time computation to help determine overall milliamp requirements.

The quick and dirty formula for this is to divide the amp hour capacity of the battery by the anticipated current flow in amps and multiply by 60 which represents the number of minutes in an hour.

Run time = battery capacity in amp hours / current in amps X 60.

For example. If your computations show you pulling 30 amps at 11.1 volts to get the wattage you desire, a 2200 mAh battery will produce an expected flight time of just over 4 minutes. Since you can't totally empty your battery plan on about 80 percent of that or 3.5 minutes. That's pretty short. How can we get longer flights? Yes, that's right, more battery capacity. Let's try a 3300 mAh battery instead. Doing the math again, we get 3.3 / 30 X 60 = 6.6 minutes. Eighty percent of that is just over 5 minutes. Still pretty short. Up the capacity again. A 5000 mAh battery should get you up to about 8 minutes using an 80% planning factor. Not too bad.

If you had been thinking about a 2200 mAh battery, the 5000 mAh battery will be much heavier. You'll probably have to examine your overall weight assumptions to make sure this much larger battery hasn't impacted your watts per pound computation and your desired performance level. If it is off by much, recompute the watts per pound to ensure you'll still get the performance you want. You may have to start the entire process again with the new and better battery weight variable.

## Online Computational Tools

Computers do math quickly and easily. As you might guess, there are several online resources available to make these computations easier. Do an online search using Google or Bing or whatever your favorite search engine is. Search on the terms 'RC motor calculator.' The results will show variety of tools. Some are web-based, others are available for download or CD purchase. Some of the web-based tools are free, others are subscription based. Some offer free trial periods or limited use versions.

The free varieties are often just basic calculators covering the simple formulas we've discussed above. Others provide more detailed results. These are usually limited by the number of products and product specifications loaded into their databases or cover just one or two manufacturers' products.

The fee-based programs are quite comprehensive. They will list dozens of not hundreds of motors, ESCs, batteries and propellers. Each component will have specific performance elements included in the database. For example, if you choose a specific motor, you'll know such things as its Kv, no-load current, resistance and other electrical measures. Rather than searching for all the technical specifications yourself, they're included in the calculator.

When you're finished entering the components you are using or thinking about using, the calculator will compute and, in some cases, chart the performance you can expect. In other cases, you can enter your model's specifics such as name, weight, wing type, desired performance level and even field elevation and the program will return a list of specific components that will meet your need.

While these tools may be a bit of overkill for the casual hobbyist, they are a great resource to serious modelers striving to get the most from their aircraft.

## Closing

Until you get into the specifics provided by the fee-based online calculators, the methods and calculations in this chapter should be viewed as 'ball park.' If you are an electrical engineer or an aspiring one, I'm sure you'll identify factors influencing total resistance or voltage drop or some other element that makes the computation off a bit one way or the other. For most of us, though, these computations will keep us from frying our motors or puffing our batteries.

As with any overview, if you can come away with an understanding of the relationships between resistance, current, voltage and power, and how to manage them, you are well on your way to understanding the basics of how your electric RC model's power system works. The good news is that there are lots of resources to help you take things to the next level if that's where your interests lie.

# 18 RC Accessories

As with any hobby or activity, there are a wide variety of accessories available to help make things easier. Some are probably more than just accessories. They're pretty much required. Others are just nifty and fun to own. Let's take a look at some of them.

## Battery Chargers

One of the required accessories an electric model aircraft flyer will need is a battery charger. Chargers that come with RTF kits usually meet the minimum requirement and usually will work only with the size and type of battery the kit comes with. One of these chargers will get you started just fine. It won't be long, however, that you'll discover you've outgrown it.

There are some features you should consider when choosing a charger. Here are some of the primary things you should consider.

## Multi-chemistry

Even inexpensive chargers can handle batteries with differing battery chemistries. You can select NiCad and NiMH, LiFe, Lipo, and lead acid (Pb). Within each type you'll have several variables you can select to ensure proper charging. For example, with lipo chemistry selected you'll be able to choose cell count or voltage and charge rate among others. Each chemistry has its own characteristics so you must carefully select your charging criteria to prevent battery damage or venting.

## Balanced Charging

Many chargers have sockets for the balance tap found on lithium batteries. Tap sizes vary according to cell count so the charger will have several sockets corresponding to the battery's cell count. Some chargers will have a small multi-wire extension connected to a small board with multiple tap sockets. This configuration will allow you to move the battery further away from the charger and allow easy use of a lipo charging sack. Others will have the sockets build into the charger itself.

Figure 18.1. A high capacity charging system powered by a large DC power supply.

Different battery brands use different balance tap configurations. That means you'll need to match your battery brand's balance tap with the charger. There are four common tap styles. TP or Thunder Power taps are used on Thunder Power batteries. JST-XH taps are used by a variety of low and mid-priced producers such as Turnigy and Zippy sold by Hobby King. JST-EH taps are less common and found on batteries sold by Graupner. Hyperion taps can be found on Hyperion batteries. As you might expect, you can find adapters or multi-brand balance boards you can plug into your charger which have connectors for various tap styles. Be sure you've matched the taps and sockets or have adapters. As discussed in the chapter on batteries, balanced charging for lipo batteries is very important for safety and long battery life.

## Wattage

Electrical power or wattage is found by multiplying current by voltage. Large battery packs can accept large charging voltages and current even at 1C. Depending on what size batteries you plan to use, you need to do a quick calculation to ensure your charger can produce the desired power. In most cases, lower cost chargers will also have lower wattage limits. For example, if you have an airplane with a 4-cell 4000 mAh battery, charging at 1C would require 14.8 volts and 4 amps. 14.8 X 4 = 59.2 watts. If your charger tops out at 50 watts, you'd have to charge at less than 1C. Protective circuitry in the charger won't allow going over the limit but the charge cycle will take longer.

## DC or AC/DC?

Most chargers are DC devices. You'll need a separate power source to power them. For modelers looking for a field charger, that often means using a DC battery. Small 12 volt sealed lead acid batteries are available for field boxes. Some modelers drag along a larger car or boat deep cycle battery to power their chargers when spending an entire day at the field.

If you have 110v AC power you can use a separate plug-in DC power supply. As with the charger itself, consider the wattage and amperage limits of the power supply when making your choice. More amps and more watts equals more cost. The flexibility of using more than one charger at a time or using small multi-battery parallel charging boards is often well worth the cost of a higher capacity power supply. More on power supplies below.

For those who don't like moving around both a charger and its power supply, you can purchase an AC/DC charger. These chargers have a built in power supply you can plug in at a field with AC power or at home. You can still hook it up to a DC source when AC isn't available.

## Multi-chargers

A very popular charger nowadays is a single unit with either two or four separate chargers built into the same case. These chargers allow you to charge several batteries at the same time. The neat thing about these chargers is that each battery can be a different size and/or chemistry. You could, for example, be charging your NiMH receiver battery while at the same time charging a small lipo for your 3D foamy and two 4-cell batteries for your warbird. Inexpensive versions of these multi-chargers will likely have a fairly low total wattage. More expensive versions allow 30 to 50 watts per channel meaning total wattage is up around 200.

## Programming and Memories

Some chargers allow several functions depending on the chemistry selected. It is not uncommon to have charge and discharge cycling for NiCad and NiMH batteries. Lipo programs may include discharge programs to drain some power from your battery, fast charge programs which omit balancing and storage programs that bring your lipo to its storage charge when it won't be used for a while.

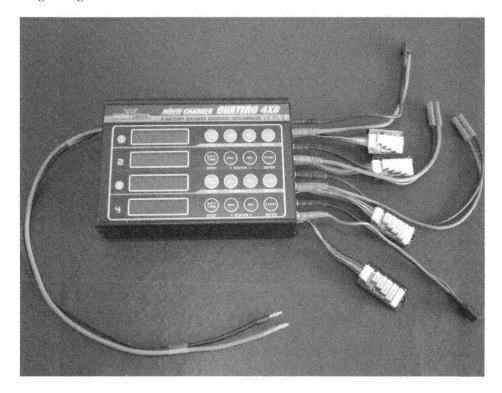

Figure 18.2. A four output multi-charger. Note both charge leads and balance boards.

Chargers may also allow you to set common settings into memories. For example, one of my chargers has 20 memories where I can set various charge rates and capacities once and then just select the memory location each time I charge that type of battery. Memories save you time and reduce the risk you'll make an input error.

## Charger Choices

At the low end of the price range are single chemistry chargers. In most cases, these chargers are built for lithium polymer batteries. You just plug them in and they charge. Some will allow you to charge a variety of small cell count packs, not just one size. The charger's circuitry senses the battery's cell count and automatically charges the cells to the correct voltage. They will normally have balance tap connectors so they can keep the battery balanced. They're normally DC devices costing less than $20.

Moving up the price continuum, you'll find basic multi-chemistry chargers. These chargers will meet the needs of many modelers. Be sure to determine if amperage or wattage limits will meet your needs. Many modelers will get several of these basic chargers and use a small 12 volt DC distribution box to power each one simultaneously. They will use them like multi-chargers but with the flexibility of just replacing one if it fails instead of losing all four to repair or replacement. These can be had for $30 to $80.

The next step up is to go with higher cost and often name brand chargers. These chargers will normally be full featured devices. They will accept multiple battery chemistries and include the programming features described above. Their big advantage is higher wattage and amperage limits. You'll need these kinds of chargers for those big five and six cell packs that power your large electric models. You can also use these high capacity chargers to power multi-battery parallel charging boards. This larger amperage and related wattage is why the large capacity charger is good for this application. High quality and high capacity chargers can easily exceed $200.

Parallel charging boards connect to the charger and have both charge and balance connections for up to six batteries. The total amperage selected at the charger should be the sum of the 1C charge rates for all connected batteries. Batteries must have the same cell counts and be discharged to approximately the same state. Total amperage must also be less than the limit of the board itself. You will need to purchase boards separately and get one that matches the connections on your batteries.

Even the small, inexpensive multi-chemistry chargers are computer controlled electrical devices. As such they have lots of options. They also have limitations. Read and follow your manufacturer's recommendations to ensure safe operation.

## Power Supplies

As mentioned above, most chargers will need a DC power source. When AC power is available, a DC power supply is a good choice. As with the charger itself, before going out and buying a power supply, consider how you plan to use it. Are you planning on using a high capacity charger? Multiple chargers? A parallel charging board? Having the answer to these questions will help you make a good choice.

Power supplies for RC modeling can be purchased from a variety of sources. Big online vendors such as Amazon will have many to choose from. Big online hobby vendors, too, will have a wide variety to choose from. I was once looking for a replacement power supply and was reminded that ham radio equipment is often powered by 12 volt power supplies. That led me to search out some specialty ham radio sources where I found a nice unit that met my needs at a reasonable price.

Most power supplies will output 13.8 volts as the standard or will be adjustable to that voltage. Chargers will normally accept a range of DC voltage from 11 volts to 15 or 18 volts. This means your 12 volt battery or 13.8 volt DC power supply will both work. For many modelers, a 13.8 volt DC output and a 30 amp capacity power supply will work well. If you are planning to use large packs or charge multiple packs at the same time, it may be worth the extra expense for a larger capacity power supply that will give you some room to grow.

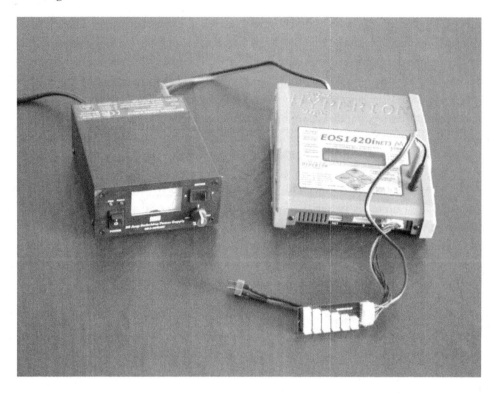

Figure 18.3. A multi-chemistry charger and DC power supply.

Just remember, as with the other electrical components in your airplanes, your power supply has limits too. If you exceed the limits you'll damage or destroy the component. Know and abide by the limits. Check your manufacturer's guidance and follow it.

## Field Boxes

You have lots of choices when it comes to field boxes. There are some boxes that are especially designed and marketed to RC flyers and some are especially made for the electric modeler. These boxes have small drawers for small pieces such as wing bolts and battery adapters. Many will have space for a hobby sized 12 volt battery and places to mount a small field charger. They will also have places for tools and other odds and ends.

Many modelers simply use tool boxes or tool bags from the big home improvement stores. These boxes come in a large variety of brands and sizes. Small boxes are great for park flyers. They provide storage for tools and batteries along with small compartments for adapters and other small items. For modelers who have greater distances to travel to get to their flying fields, many choose to go with large or very larges tool boxes. They'll put everything they can think of into their portable workshops allowing them to fix or replace damaged items to extend the flying day even after a crash.

Your field box should contain a variety of screw drivers, various sized hex wrenches, battery adapters, battery balance and status tools, glues and an adjustable wrench that fits your propeller nuts. Extra propellers and small parts such as wheel collars are also a good idea. One good idea for the beginning modeler is to get a multi-bit precision screwdriver set. A starter set at Harbor Freight will set you back only $6 - $7. That set will cover phillips heads, common heads and hex heads. A precision sized set of needle nose pliers cost about the same. Last, find a couple of hemostats to reach into the tight places that things always seem to fall.

You'll also need a case for your radio. Likewise for your power supply and charger if they go along to the field. They, too, can fit into tool boxes. I particularly like the cases that come with dividers and are filled with foam blocks that can be easily configured to fit whatever I plan to put in them. Amazon and Harbor Freight are both good sources.

## Battery Boxes

As we've discussed already, lipo batteries can be hazardous if not treated properly. Having a safe way to transport your batteries both to and from the field is important. Having six or eight batteries sitting in a cardboard shoe box doesn't meet that criteria.

If you fly with just a couple of fairly small batteries, you can use a fireproof box marketed to keep your important documents safe at home. These boxes can hold several batteries and are lockable. Another popular choice is to visit your local military surplus store and pick up a couple of metal ammo boxes. These boxes clean up well and can be painted in your favorite 'rattle can' color. Even in their natural green finish, they'll do the trick. Some recommend drilling a couple of small holes in the lid in case a battery flares up. The small opening will allow pressure and gases to vent while containing most of the fire and heat.

One suggestion is to have 'charged' and 'discharged' boxes. You can take your charged batteries to the field in one and your spent batteries back home in the other. Another idea is to have a second (or third) box to transport a seriously puffed or damaged battery back home for proper disposal. Tossing a damaged battery into the trash is dangerous. Take it home in your safety container.

## Watt Meter

As mentioned in Chapter 8, one of the first RC gadgets an electric modeler needs to have is a watt meter. These small devices plug in between the model's battery and ESC. As the throttle is advanced the watt meter will display key data. Most watt meters will display information in each corner of the display.

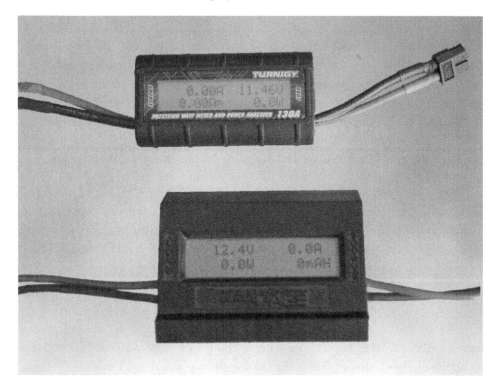

Figure 18.4. Different brands of watt meters. A critical tool for the electric modeler.

One data element will be voltage. As you know, voltage is one of the key measures for computing wattage. Another data element will be amps. Amps is the second element in computing wattage. With those two identified the third element will be wattage. The last displayed element is amp hours.

The voltage reading can give you some insight into the battery's ability to power your model. Voltage under load can go down drastically in batteries that are failing. This number will help you keep an eye on overall battery health.

The amperage reading helps ensure you don't exceed amperage limits on the power system's components. Batteries, ESCs and motors all have amp limits. Any time you change propellers you should recheck the amp reading using your watt meter.

The wattage reading will give you an idea of the performance you can expect from your model. We described the various watts per pound of model weight recommendations in Chapter 17. Your watt meter will display the wattage and you can do the math to see whether you'll have that full unlimited vertical or not. Your motor may also have a published watt limit. You'll be able to see if you're within limits on that too.

The amp hour reading is probably the least used display. This display shows the amp hours used. One use for this data is to note the amp hour reading at a particular throttle setting to compute an estimated flight time at that setting. We discussed the formula earlier in Chapter 17. In this case, instead of using the full amperage rating of the circuit, you can compute flight times at lower throttle settings and their accompanying lower current flows.

## Battery Checkers

There are several styles of battery checkers on the market. Many appear to be the same devices with just different branding. These are also important tools for the electric modeler. These little boxes will allow you to connect your battery via the balance tap and receive important data about the status of your battery.

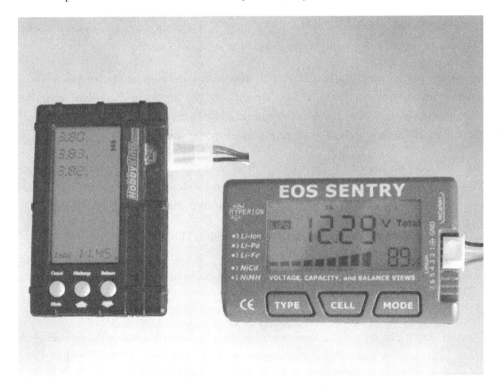

Figure 18.5. Battery checkers come in a variety shapes and sizes.

Most of these checkers will display both total voltage and voltage by cell. This allows you to see whether the pack is discharging in a balanced fashion. Remember that each of the battery's cells is an independent element. They can and do fail independently. One indicator is when one cell consistently discharges more deeply than the other cells in the pack. Many of these checkers also have balancing circuits so you can leave the battery connected to the checker and it will try to balance the cells before you put the pack back on the charger.

One of my favorite battery checkers is the EOS Battery Sentry. I use it after every flight to check on the condition of my battery. I particularly like how it displays battery capacity as a percentage, not just remaining voltage. At a glance I can determine how much is left and adjust my flying time appropriately. I shoot for a post flight reading of about 25%.

Many checkers will allow you to select between several battery chemistries. In so doing, the checker will display results based on each cell's voltage depending on its chemistry. Only batteries with balance taps can display data by cell.

## Clothing

RC flying is primarily an outdoor sport. You'll want to have clothing for the typical weather in the area you live. You'll want to dress in layers allowing you to shed clothing as the day progresses or to add layers if the forecast is for cooling.

One critical fashion item is a hat. Hats with wide brims will help keep your face and neck shaded from the sun's rays and all the damage they can do. Some flyers like to use hats with capes down the back to cover their necks. The fishing department at your favorite sporting goods store is a good place to find a hat you'll enjoy wearing.

Your shoes are an important item too. Sandals and flip flops are not the best choices. There are dropped tools, sharp propeller blades and walks through the brush to retrieve downed models. Plan on wearing good athletic shoes or hikers to protect your feet.

The last item isn't technically clothing, it's sunscreen. Those beautiful summer days out at the flying field means lots of sun exposure. Use high SPF rated sunscreen to protect yourself from the damaging effects of the sun and those scary skin cancers.

## Closing

There are entire catalogs of RC tools and gadgets. This short list doesn't even scratch the surface. Part of the fun will be looking through the magazine ads and online hobby superstores thinking about that special gadget you just have to add to your collection.

The ones listed are a good place to start. These items will get you started without breaking the bank. They will help you manage the health of your various components or make sure you've got them protected.

## ABOUT THE AUTHOR

Jim Mohan is a long time modeler, educator and trainer. Jim's aviation experience includes a twenty-year career as an Air Force pilot, instructor pilot, classroom trainer and curriculum manager. He has also been an adjunct professor at the community college, undergraduate and graduate levels. He has been engaged in flying electric models exclusively for the past ten years. He has a YouTube channel dedicated to building and flying electric model aircraft.

Please visit his web page at www.rcplaneviews.com. It has reviews of some of his planes and other RC products as well as videos and photos. It also has links to his blog and companion learning site. If you have comments on this book you can email him at jim@rcplaneviews.com.

Made in the USA
Coppell, TX
13 January 2025

44351861R00085